Inspirations

Inspirations

Selected with an Introduction

by PAULO COELHO

PENGUIN CLASSICS
an imprint of
PENGUIN BOOKS

PENGUIN CLASSICS

Published by the Penguin Group
Penguin Books Ltd, 80 Strand, London WC2R 0RL, England
Penguin Group (USA) Inc., 375 Hudson Street, New York, New York 10014, USA
Penguin Group (Canada), 90 Eglinton Avenue East, Suite 700, Toronto, Ontario, Canada M4P 2Y3
(a division of Pearson Penguin Canada Inc.)
Penguin Ireland, 25 St Stephen's Green, Dublin 2, Ireland (a division of Penguin Books Ltd)
Penguin Group (Australia), 250 Camberwell Road, Camberwell, Victoria 3124, Australia
(a division of Pearson Australia Group Pty Ltd)
Penguin Books India Pvt Ltd, 11 Community Centre, Panchsheel Park, New Delhi – 110 017, India
Penguin Group (NZ), 67 Apollo Drive, Rosedale, North Shore 0632, New Zealand
(a division of Pearson New Zealand Ltd)
Penguin Books (South Africa) (Pty) Ltd, 24 Sturdee Avenue, Rosebank,
Johannesburg 2196, South Africa

Penguin Books Ltd, Registered Offices: 80 Strand, London WC2R 0RL, England

www.penguin.com

This selection first published 2010

4

Selection and introduction copyright © Paulo Coelho, 2010

The moral right of the editor has been asserted

The Acknowledgements on pp. 237–40 constitute an extension of this page.

Set in 12/14.5pt Monotype Fournier
Typeset by Palimpsest Book Production Limited, Grangemouth, Stirlingshire
Printed in Great Britain by Clays Ltd, St Ives plc

A CIP catalogue record for this book is available from the British Library

HARDBACK ISBN: 978-1-846-14197-3
TRADE PAPERBACK ISBN: 978-0-141-19400-4

www.greenpenguin.co.uk

Consider the lilies of the field, how they grow; they toil not,
neither do they spin: And yet I say unto you, That even
Solomon in all his glory was not arrayed like one of these.

(Matt. 6:28—9)

Contents

Preface   xi

WATER

Subtle Realm – Unconsciousness – Mind – Dreams –
Strategy – Logic – Possibilities – Passivity – Mobility

Introduction   3
Hans Christian Andersen: *The Ugly Duckling*   5
'The Prologue' from *Tales from the Thousand and*
     One Nights   15
Niccolò Machiavelli: from *The Prince*   23
Lewis Carroll: from *Through the Looking-Glass –*
     'Looking-glass House'   43
Sun-tzu: from *The Art of War* – 'Forms and
     Dispositions'   53

EARTH

Winter – Body – Decay – Womb – Mother – Receptive –
Passive – Stagnation (Prison) – Roots

Introduction   61
Oscar Wilde: from *De Profundis*   63
Bram Stoker: from *Dracula* –
     'Dr Seward's Diary'   76
Hannah Arendt: from *Eichmann and*
     the Holocaust   81

Contents

W. B. Yeats: from *Selected Poems* – 'He wishes for
the Cloths of Heaven' and 'The Song of Wandering
Aengus'   90
D. H. Lawrence: from *Lady Chatterley's Lover*   92

AIR

*Breath – Life – Communication – Action – Instability –
Agitation (not action)*

Introduction   107
Nelson Mandela: from *No Easy Walk to Freedom* –
'Black Man in a White Man's Court'   109
Gabriel García Márquez: from *One Hundred Years
of Solitude*   117
Robert Louis Stevenson: from *The Strange Case of
Dr Jekyll and Mr Hyde* – 'Henry Jekyll's Full
Statement of the Case'   125
George Orwell: from *Nineteen Eighty-Four*   132
Jorge Luis Borges: from *Fictions* – 'The Library
of Babel'   141

FIRE

*Spirit – Light – Heat – Darkness (Smoke) Hymn –
Hell – Motion: Root of all change*

Introduction   153
From the *Rig Veda* – 'Hymns to Agni, God of
the Sacrifice'   156
From *The Desert Fathers* – Sayings of the Early
Christian Monks – 'Visions'   167
From the *Bhagavad Gita*   181
From the *Dead Sea Scrolls*   192
Leopold Sacher-Masoch: from *Venus in Furs*   194
Kahlil Gibran: from *The Prophet*   199
Rumi: from *Spiritual Verses*   202

Contents

Rabindranath Tagore: from *Selected Poems* —
  'Brahmā, Viṣṇu, Śiva'   223
Mary Shelley: from *Frankenstein*   227

Acknowledgements   237

Preface

A few months back a friend of mine sent me a little book by the Argentinian writer Jorge Luis Borges entitled *The Book*. In fact, it is the transcription of a talk Borges gave towards the end of his life (1978). This great writer had already lost his vision by the time he 'composed' this text and that's why the small book I received has the fluidity and closeness of a talk that he probably gave in the dark study of his flat in Buenos Aires – an interesting talk that I wish I could have had with him in an Argentinian café of the neighbourhood of Recoleta or towards the Plaza de Mayo in Buenos Aires. The reason I mention this event is because – like all miracles in life – this strange little book appeared in my life at the exact moment I had this anthology to compile and it talks precisely about the moment when the written word surpassed the oral message in our culture.

Borges starts his talk by saying how the Ancients did not revere the book – the written word – as we do. Rather, they saw in the written word a sort of imprisonment of the spirit, of oral teachings. Indeed, to write a message down transforms it: it becomes visible, palpable and no longer dwells in the space between the speaker and the listener. The message becomes 'heavier', acquires a body of ink and paper (or clay in ancient times) and is supposed to live longer than the person who first spoke it. Borges observes that most of the great teachers of ancient times wrote not a single word. The teachings of Buddha, Pythagoras, Socrates or Lao Tzu were all oral, their students being the ones to write them down. Jesus follows the same path – yet with this striking difference that he, once, wrote in words in the sand that were soon blown away by the wind.

To write was the artifice the apprentices had to resort to in order to record the message of these great men. Writing emerges then as an extension of memory.

Of course, the Torah as well as the Koran or the Indian Vedas are exceptions, given that they are holy books, believed to have been written by God himself. For the Hindus the *Rig Veda* is 'non-human', has always existed and only appears at a precise time of a cycle. The text then that we have inaugurates our manifested world. The Torah and the Koran both capture the very breath of God. In this case, there is an inversion of the perception of the book: from a mere transcription, the written word becomes spirit itself, the beating heart of a religion. Every page, every line, every word, every letter carries the mark of an endless memory, of a bottomless knowledge.

Yet, these sacred books – because they are written – represent the idea of an extension of memory. One has simply to remember the scene in which God inscribed the Ten Commandments in stone to understand that we humans need these divine 'memoranda'.

It becomes clear that the written word enables us to remember, but at the same time it perpetuates this loss of memory – we no longer need to make the effort of remembering since it's written down. Plato, in the *Phaedrus*, puts a story in Socrates' mouth that is quite telling of this very contradiction.

But why am I mentioning all this? An anthology – I came to discover – comes from the Greek words meaning a flower-gathering – in other words, a bouquet of flowers. An anthology, then, would be a sort of reminder of something else, a small token of something much larger. Flowers bring with their fragrance and colour a reminder of the fields, of a season. An anthology, if I am to follow Borges' logic, is a reminder of other books that, in their turn, are reminders of an oral, living message.

An anthology is not only a collection of texts or poems, but a gift, something we arrange, according to our sensitivities, to give to others. The flowers themselves are not created by us – in this case, the books that I choose to present to you lie in front of me as a vast field of flowers, stretching infinitely into time's horizon. To push this idea a little bit further: some of these texts, such as the *Rig Veda* or the Dead Sea Scrolls, are not attributable to a specific single writer, but to this common furnace of imagination that lights humanity.

At the beginning of my work, I decided to stroll in this beautiful field. I remember having to choose from the vast collection of Penguin Classics and feeling that what lay ahead of me was of titanic proportions. Imagine: from the *Rig Veda* to *Lady Chatterley* – how could I possibly make any sense of the great variety of books that throughout my life have fed my imagination? Let's be honest – throughout a lifetime we amass a quantity of stories and information that only our forgetfulness puts into shape. It is like the work of a sculptor who, with his chisel and mallet, chips away at the excesses of the stone in order to reveal his creation.

Forgetfulness, then, moulded my memory and when I started to venture into these golden fields, little by little scenes, words, visions came back to me. Suddenly I felt I was no longer out in the open air, but revisiting a personal garden.

Yet, even though I found a renewed pleasure while turning the pages of these books, I still had to face the hardest part: to present all this richness to you. Where to start? How to make head or tail of such a diversity of texts? More difficult still: how would I choose the passages?

Borges in his talk mentions Emerson, who used to say that a library was like a magic cabinet. In books we find the best demonstrations of the human spirit, but in order for them to come to life, we need to open them and read them. In the case of this anthology I will be presenting glimpses of these great spirits, and my aim with this work is that readers will feel compelled to go to their magic cabinets and re-awaken their imagination.

But if the aim is clear and natural, how to get there, on the other hand, is not so easy. Firstly, there are countless ways of arranging texts together. Some of these methods appear more dispassionate than others, such as the possibility of grouping texts chronologically, alphabetically, by geographical areas, etc. . . . At first, this seemed the safest bet since the reader would quickly be able to find out who the writers were and when they wrote. Yet presenting this knowledge – this outward information – didn't convince me.

I felt this would be like making a bouquet with no true originality – putting different flowers together simply because they start with the same letter or are the same height. Imagine offering a bouquet with flowers whose names started with the letter R – we would end up with quite a messy gift, handing over a muddled mass of Ranunculus, Raspberries, Reeds, Rhubarb, Roses, Rosemary, Rue and Rye-grass. Where is the invention in that? It certainly would be a fun thing to do (I'm sure Jacques Prévert, the French poet, with his endless lists would be carried away by this) but I'm not sure if each flower would quite stand out and the fragrance of each species be clearly distinct.

While thinking about this I remembered Ikebana – the Japanese art of flower arrangement. In Japan, bouquets are not thought of in the same way as in the west – the Japanese concentrate more on the lines and spaces between the flowers rather than on the colours and fulness of these arrangements. That's why, when carefully selecting the material, they never combine too many species of flowers. They also give particular importance to the leaves – as if these were the necessary spaces to reveal the essence of colours and the purity of the composition.

Ikebana is not simply about aesthetics – it is also part of the Zen tradition and is therefore a form of meditation, as is Kyudo (archery) or calligraphy. When Chinese Buddhist monks were introducing Ikebana into Japan in the sixth century, they would create arrangements to be offered in the temples, and these offerings were put together in such a way that the eyes of the viewers would be lifted up by the composition. These bouquets were in a way a sort of natural cathedral that aimed at stirring the soul of the viewers and paying homage to Buddha.

While reading about Ikebana, I also discovered that these sacred bouquets were arranged according to three main lines that symbolized heaven, earth and humankind. This relation between the elements brought me back to a familiar idea: the ancient notion of the four elements.

The Ancients believed that all things – visible and invisible – were composed of four different substances, uncreated and imperishable: Earth, Water, Air and Fire. It's important to stress that these elements were not simply considered in their material form – they were in fact understood symbolically. The attributes of each element then corresponded to a specific spiritual, mental or physical dimension.

Thus, the elemental air is not only the air, but a temper, a way to behave, bringing back specific colours and smells, portraying a particular universe. Elemental water goes far beyond the sea or the oceans, lakes and pools to reach a dominion of beautiful dreams, possibilities and ideas. The Greek philosopher Empedocles, who lived sometime in the fifth century BC, is the one who proposed a precise theory of the four elements, and, after him, Aristotle made it a pillar of his philosophical system. The theory of the elements was a great success in Antiquity as well as during the Middle Ages, both in the east and in the west.

But in fact this theory goes far back into an immemorial past and presents itself as a basis for meditation and science. It seems strange to us because when we see fire, for instance, we just see fire and nothing else. The Ancients saw many other things because each material object was a symbolic key leading to a more complete reality, a reality that, though invisible, ruled everyday life.

The four elements symbolize both our world in all its dimensions and the way we dwell in this world, the way we see it.

Many stories can be summed up in a few tales. Storytelling can be understood as a wonderful and powerful crystal that grows deep in the narrator's mind and heart to flourish in words and images.

Let me briefly introduce to you the four main parts of this book as if I were describing beautiful flowers. But may those special flowers, instead of withering and perishing, grow and blossom, again and again, in your lives . . .

Let's imagine a circle made out of those four elements. They make a wheel, a vivid wheel spinning over the world and in its innermost part: our hearts. If a traveller could travel to the end of the world, he might discover this wheel turning in front of him and within him. And he would be complete, as one. Indeed, those four elements form an idea of the whole, of the universe. To feel complete, as a being, can be a very difficult task. And an anthology like this one can never be complete until, reader, it is read by you. And your insight completes the circle and makes it turn again.

Like this traveller, let us go to the end of the world, to gaze at those elements scattered in the heavens. And what will be the first journey?

WATER

Introduction

Water. Deep water. Infinitely deep water of the primordial ocean, where everything is possible. It is the origin of the world, an ocean far bigger and wider than what we see on earth. Something huge and fantastic, bottomless. It is the return to a kind of dissolution, with all its dangers, and the chance for a new birth. We can find horrid monsters and fascinating creatures in the depths of the water. The liquid cannot support us, but we know that life itself first appeared in water. The unconscious life dwells here, the deepest desires form like fishes in the darkest part of the ocean and then rise towards the light, where they can transform themselves into new dreams and ideas. Water was linked to the 'lymphatic' temper in ancient medicine, to signify a sort of calm but rather passive temperament. Of course, our body and the world are bound together by myriads of subtle links and correspondences. The following texts illustrate this in their own ways.

With *The Ugly Duckling*, by Hans Christian Andersen, we confront the awkwardness of a different life among more 'normal' lives, and the struggle to affirm something worthwhile. Then, with the beginning of *The Thousand and One Nights*, we hear the whimsical story of Shahrazad and her tormented destiny: because she was supposed to die, she invented a strategy to survive. Water is likewise imagination and invention, the very deep root of our mind that can reveal to us many treasures. Those treasures, unfortunately, can be ambiguous. Machiavelli's *The Prince* illustrates how fear itself can be a valuable tool in some situations. Fear, like those unknown monsters from the deep, can show us how strength is often linked to the stranger parts of the human being. Lewis Carroll's *Through the Looking-Glass* tells us that reality can be slightly different from how we usually think about it. And the expression, 'to walk through the looking-glass', is now commonly used to explain how the way we perceive reality can be altered, sometimes in its own way, and without us. *The Art of War*, by Sun-tzu, provides us with enigmatic and puzzling advice. The ground, or the earth, is called forth, but water lies like a sort of reminder – a reminder of the origins of mind and the very basis of will.

HANS CHRISTIAN ANDERSEN

The Ugly Duckling

It was so lovely out in the country. It was summer. The rye was yellow, the oats green, the hay had been gathered in stacks down in the green meadows. That's where the stork was walking around on his long red legs, speaking Egyptian, because that was the language he had learned from his mother. Surrounding the fields and meadows were great forests, and in the middle of the forests were deep lakes. Oh yes, it was truly lovely out in the country! In the midst of the sunshine stood an old estate with a deep moat all around. From the walls and down to the water grew huge dock leaves that were so tall that little children could stand upright under the largest of them. It was just as wild in there as in the thickest forest, and this was where a duck was sitting on her nest. She had to sit there to hatch her little ducklings, but now she was getting tired of it all because it was taking such a long time, and she rarely had visitors. The other ducks were more fond of swimming around in the moat than running over to sit under a dock leaf to chat with her.

Finally one egg cracked open after the other. 'Peep! Peep!' they said. All the egg yolks had come alive and were sticking out their heads.

'Quack! Quack!' she said, and they all rushed out as fast as they could and looked all around under the green leaves. Their mother let them look as much as they liked, because green is good for the eyes.

'How big the world is!' said all the youngsters, because now they had quite a bit more room than when they were lying inside the eggs.

'You think this is the whole world?' said their mother. 'It stretches far away to the other side of the garden, all the way to the pastor's field, although I've never been that far. But you're all here now, aren't you?' And then she got up. 'No, I don't have all of you. The biggest egg is still lying here. How long is it going to take? I'm getting very tired of this!' And then she sat down again.

'So, how's it going?' said an old duck who came to visit.

'One egg is taking such a long time,' said the duck on the nest. 'It won't crack open. But take a look at the others. They're the loveliest ducklings I've ever seen! They all look like their father, that rogue who never comes to see me.'

'Let me look at the egg that won't crack open,' said the old duck. 'I'll bet it's a turkey egg! I was once fooled like that myself, and I had my share of troubles with those youngsters, because they're afraid of the water, let me tell you. I couldn't get them to go in. I quacked and snapped, but it did no good. Let me see that egg. It's a turkey egg, all right! Just leave it here and go teach the other children to swim.'

'I think I'll sit on it for a while longer,' said the duck. 'I've been sitting here this long, I might as well sit here the rest of the summer.'

'Be my guest,' said the old duck, and then she left.

Finally the big egg cracked open. 'Peep! Peep!' said the youngster and tumbled out. He was so big and hideous. The duck looked at him. 'That's certainly an awfully big duckling,' she said. 'None of the others look like that. He couldn't be a turkey chick, could he? Well, we shall soon see! Into the water he goes, even if I have to kick him in myself.'

The next day the weather was gloriously beautiful. The sun shone on all the green dock plants. The mother duck and her whole family went down to the moat. Splash! She jumped into the water. 'Quack! Quack!' she said, and one duckling after the other plopped in. The water washed over their heads, but they popped up at once and floated around so beautifully. Their legs moved on their own and all of them were in the water; even the hideous grey youngster was swimming along.

'No, he's not a turkey,' she said. 'Look how beautifully he uses his legs, how erect he holds himself! That's my child! Actually he's quite handsome if you take a good look. Quack! Quack! Come along with me, and I'll take you out into the world and introduce you to the duck yard. But stay close to me so that no one steps on you, and watch out for the cats.'

And then they went into the duck yard. There was a terrible ruckus going on because two families were fighting over an eel head, and then the cat ended up getting it.

'See, that's how things go in the world,' said the mother duck, licking her bill, because she too would have liked to have had that eel head. 'Use your legs now,' she said. 'See if you can't hurry it up, and dip your necks to the old duck over there. She's the most refined of anyone here. She has Spanish blood, that's why she's so fat. And see there: she has a red rag around her leg. That's a remarkably lovely thing and the highest honour any duck can be given. She's so important that they won't get rid of her, and both animals and humans must respect her. Hurry up! Don't put your legs together. A well-mannered duckling keeps his legs far apart, just like Father and Mother. Come on! Now dip your neck and say, "Quack!"'

And that's what they did. But the other ducks standing around looked at them and said quite loudly, 'Look at this! Now we've got to deal with that bunch too. As if there weren't enough of us already. And ugh, just take a look at that duckling! We're not going to put up with him!' And one of the ducks flew over and promptly bit him on the back of the neck.

'Leave him alone!' said the mother. 'He's not hurting anyone!'

'Yes, but he's too big and too odd looking,' said the duck who had bitten him. 'So he's going to be pushed around.'

'What handsome children that mother has!' said the old duck with the rag around her leg. 'All of them so handsome except for one; that one certainly didn't turn out too well. I wish she could hatch that one over again.'

'That's not possible, Your Grace,' said the mother duck. 'He may not be handsome, but he has a genuinely good nature, and he swims as beautifully as any of the others; yes, I'd venture to say even a little better. I think he'll be handsome when he grows up, or with time he might get a little smaller. He was too long in the egg, and that's why he isn't the right shape.' Then she plucked at the back of his neck and smoothed out his feathers. 'Besides, he's a drake,' she said, 'so it doesn't matter as much. I think he'll turn out to be strong, and I'm sure he'll win a place for himself.'

'The other ducklings are so charming,' said the old duck. 'Make yourselves at home, and if you happen to find an eel head, you can bring it to me.'

And so they made themselves at home.

But the poor duckling who was the last to come out of his egg and looked so horrid was bitten, shoved and teased by both the ducks and the hens. 'He's too big,' they all said. And the tom turkey, who was born with spurs, which made him think he was an emperor, puffed himself up like a ship at full sail, walked right over to him, and started gobbling until he turned bright red in the face. The poor duckling had no idea which way to turn. He was very sad because he looked so hideous and was ridiculed by the whole duck yard.

That's how it went on the first day, and afterward it got worse and worse. The poor duckling was chased by everyone. Even his siblings were mean to him, and they always said, 'If only the cat would get you! What a horrid troublemaker you are!' And his mother said, 'If only you were far away!' The ducks bit him, and the hens pecked at him, and the maid who was supposed to feed the animals gave him a kick with her foot.

Then he took off running and flew over the hedge. The little birds in the bushes darted up into the air out of fright. 'It's because I'm so hideous,' thought the duckling and closed his eyes but still kept on running. Then he reached the great marsh where the wild ducks lived. There he lay all night, he was so tired and sad.

In the morning the wild ducks flew up, and they looked at their new companion. 'Who on earth are you?' they asked, and the duckling turned this way and that, greeting them as best he could.

'You're awfully hideous,' said the wild ducks. 'But that doesn't matter to us, provided you don't marry anyone in our family.' The poor thing! He had no intention of getting married, as long as he was allowed to sit among the reeds and drink a little marsh water.

There he stayed for two whole days. Then two wild geese came along, or rather two wild ganders, because they were males. It wasn't long ago that they had come out of their eggs, and that's why they were so brash.

'Listen here, my friend,' they said. 'You're so hideous that we actually like you! Want to come along and be a migrating bird? Nearby, in another marsh, there are some heavenly sweet wild geese, all of them young ladies who could say, "Quack!" You're in a position to be a success, because you're so hideous.'

'Bang! Boom!' they suddenly heard overhead. Both the wild geese fell dead into the reeds, and the water turned blood-red. Bang! Boom! was heard again, and entire flocks of wild geese rose up from the reeds. Then shots rang out again. A great hunt was under way. The hunters lay all around the marsh. Some were even up in the tree branches that stretched far out over the reeds. Blue smoke drifted like clouds among the dark trees and hovered far out over the water. Through the mud came the hunting dogs. Splash! Splash! Reeds and rushes swayed on all sides. What a horror it was for the poor duckling! He turned his head to tuck it under his wing, but just at that moment a huge terrifying dog stopped right next to him, his long tongue hanging out of his mouth and his eyes shining horridly. He lowered his jaws toward the duckling, showed his sharp teeth and . . . Splish! Splish! He left without taking him.

'Oh, thank God,' sighed the duckling. 'I'm so hideous that not even the dog wanted to bite me.'

And he lay very still as the bullets whistled through the reeds, with one shot exploding after the other.

Not until late in the day was it quiet, but the poor youngster still didn't dare stand up. He waited another few hours before he looked around and then hurried away from the marsh as fast as he could, racing over field and meadow. There was a strong wind, so he had a hard time making headway.

Toward evening he reached a poor little farmhouse. It was so wretched that it couldn't make up its mind which way to fall, and that's why it was still standing. The wind was blowing so hard against the duckling that he had to sit on his tail to hold his ground, and it got worse and worse. Then he noticed that the door had come loose from one of its hinges and was hanging so crookedly that he could slip through the crack into the house, and that's what he did.

Inside lived an old woman with her cat and her hen. The cat, who was called Sonny, could arch his back and purr. He could even throw off sparks, but for that you had to stroke his fur the wrong way. The hen had very short little legs, and that's why she was called 'Henny Shortlegs'. She was good at laying eggs, and the woman was as fond of her as of her own child.

In the morning they noticed at once the strange duckling. The cat started purring and the hen began to cluck.

'What's this?' said the woman, looking all around, but she couldn't see well, and that's why she thought the duckling was a plump duck that had gone astray. 'What a nice find,' she said. 'Now I can have duck eggs, if only it's not a drake. We'll have to give it a try.'

And so the duckling was accepted on a trial basis for three weeks, but no eggs appeared. The cat was master of the house, and the hen was the mistress. They both kept on saying, '*We* and the rest of the world,' because they thought they were half of it, and the better half at that. The duckling thought it might be possible to have another opinion, but the hen wouldn't stand for it.

'Can you lay eggs?' she asked.

'No.'

'Well then, you'd better keep your mouth shut!'

And the cat said, 'Can you arch your back, purr and throw sparks?'

'No.'

'Well then, we don't want to hear from you when sensible people are talking!'

And the duckling sat in the corner, in a bad temper. Then he happened to think about the fresh air and sunshine. He had such a strange desire to float on the water that at last he couldn't resist, he had to tell the hen.

'What's come over you?' she asked. 'You don't have anything to do, that's why you get such ideas into your head. Lay eggs or purr, and it will pass.'

'But it's so lovely to float on the water,' said the duckling. 'So lovely to dip your head under water and dive down to the bottom.'

'Oh, that's a great pleasure, all right!' said the hen. 'You must be crazy! Ask the cat – and he's the smartest one I know – whether he likes floating on the water or diving underneath. I won't even talk about myself. Or you can ask our mistress, the old woman. There's no one wiser than her in the whole world. Do you think she wants to float and get water on her head?'

'You don't understand me,' said the duckling.

'Well, if we don't understand you, then who does? You'll never be smarter than the cat or the old woman, not to mention myself. Stop making a fuss, child! And thank your Creator for all the kindness that has been shown to you. Haven't you ended up in a warm house, with companions that you can learn something from? But you're a fool, and it's not amusing to be around you. Believe me, it's for your own good that I'm telling you these unpleasant things. That's how you know who your true friends are. So see to it that you lay eggs and learn to purr and throw sparks.'

'I think I'll go out into the wide world,' said the duckling.

'Well, go ahead!' said the hen.

And so the duckling left. He floated on the water, then dove down, but all the animals ignored him because he was ugly.

Then autumn came, the leaves in the forest turned brown and yellow, the wind seized hold of them so they danced around, and the sky looked cold. The clouds hung heavy with hail and snowflakes, and on the fence stood a raven, shrieking 'Ow! Ow!' from sheer cold. Yes, you could end up freezing just by thinking about it. Things certainly weren't going well for the poor duckling.

One evening as the sun was setting gloriously, a whole flock of lovely big birds came out of the thickets. The duckling had never seen anything so beautiful. They were a dazzling white, with long supple necks. They were swans. They uttered quite a wondrous sound, spread out their magnificent long wings, and flew away from the cold regions to the warmer countries, to open waters. They climbed so high, so high, and the little ugly duckling felt quite strange. He spun around in the water like a wheel, stretching his neck high up into the air after them, uttering a cry so loud and strange that it scared even him. Oh, he couldn't forget those lovely birds, those happy birds. As soon as he lost sight of them, he dove straight down to the bottom, and when he came back up, he was practically beside himself. He didn't know what those birds were called or where they were flying, but he loved them as he had never loved anyone else. He didn't envy them in the least; how could he even think of wishing for such loveliness? He would have been happy if the ducks had merely allowed him to stay among them. The poor ugly creature!

And the winter was so cold, so cold. The duckling had to swim around in the water to keep it from freezing over. But every night the hole in which he was swimming grew smaller and smaller. It froze so hard that the icy crust crackled. The duckling had to keep moving his legs or the water would close up. At last he grew so weak that he lay quite still and then was frozen into the ice.

Early in the morning a farmer appeared. He saw the duckling, went out, smashed the ice to bits with his wooden clog, and carried the bird home to his wife. There the duckling was revived.

The children wanted to play with him, but the duckling thought they were trying to hurt him and flew in terror right into the milk basin so the milk splashed all over the room. The farmer's wife screamed and flapped her hands in the air. Then the duckling flew into the trough of butter and then into the flour barrel and out again. What a sight he was! The farmer's wife screamed and swung at him with the hearth tongs, and the children tumbled all over each other to catch the duckling, as they laughed and shrieked. It was a good thing that the door stood open. Out he rushed into the bushes in the newly fallen snow. There he lay, as if in a daze.

But it would be much too sad to recount all the suffering and misery he had to endure that harsh winter. He was lying in the marsh among the rushes when the sunshine once again began to feel warm. The larks sang. It was lovely springtime.

Then all of a sudden he lifted his wings; they flapped stronger than before and powerfully carried him away. And before he even knew it, he was in a great garden where the apple trees stood in bloom, where the lilacs hung fragrantly on their long green boughs all the way down to the winding waterways. Oh, it was so lovely there, so springtime fresh! And right in front of him, out of the thickets, came three lovely white swans. They ruffled their feathers and floated so lightly on the water. The duckling recognized the magnificent creatures and was stirred by a strange sadness.

'I'll fly over to them, those royal birds. And they'll peck me to death because someone like me, who is so hideous, dares approach them. But it doesn't matter! Better to be killed by them than to be nipped by the ducks, pecked by the hens, kicked by the maid who tends the chicken coops, and to suffer so terribly all winter.' And be flew out into the water and swam over to the magnificent swans. They saw him and came gliding toward him with ruffled feathers. 'Go ahead and kill me!' said the poor bird, and he bent his head down to the surface of the water and waited for death. But what did he see in the clear water? He saw beneath him his own image, and he was no longer a clumsy, greyish-black bird, horrid and hideous. He was a swan!

It doesn't matter if you're born in a duck yard when you've been lying inside a swan's egg.

He actually felt glad about all the suffering and hardships he had endured. Now he could appreciate his happiness and all the loveliness that awaited him. And the great swans swam all around him, stroking him with their bills.

Several little children came into the garden. They threw bread and grain into the water, and the youngest of them cried, 'There's a new one!'

And the other children also shouted joyfully, 'Yes, a new one has arrived!' And they clapped their hands and danced around. They ran to find Father and Mother. Bread and cakes were tossed into the water, and they all said, 'The new one is the most beautiful of all! So young and so lovely!' And the old swans bowed to him.

Then he felt quite bashful and tucked his head behind his wings. He didn't know what to make of it. He was much too happy, but not the least bit proud, because a good heart is never proud. He thought about how he had been badgered and scorned, and now he heard everyone say that he was the loveliest of all the lovely birds. The lilacs dipped their boughs all the way down to him in the water, and the sun shone so warm and so fine. Then he ruffled his feathers, raised his slender neck, and rejoiced with all his heart. 'I never dreamed of so much happiness when I was the ugly duckling!'

Tales from the Thousand and One Nights

The Prologue

The Tale of King Shahriyar and his Brother Shahzaman

It is related – but Allah alone is wise and all-knowing – that long ago there lived in the lands of India and China a Sassanid king who commanded great armies and had numerous courtiers, followers and servants. He left two sons, both renowned for their horsemanship – especially the elder, who inherited the kingdom of his father and governed it with such justice that all his subjects loved him. He was called King Shahriyar. His younger brother was named Shahzaman and was king of Samarkand.

The two brothers continued to reign happily in their kingdoms, and after a period of twenty years King Shahriyar felt a great longing to see his younger brother. He ordered his Vizier to go to Samarkand and invite him to his court.

The Vizier set out promptly on his mission and journeyed many days and nights through deserts and wildernesses until he arrived at Shahzaman's city and was admitted to his presence. He gave him King Shahriyar's greetings and informed him of his master's wish to see him. King Shahzaman was overjoyed at the prospect of visiting his brother. He made ready to leave his kingdom, and sent out his tents, camels, mules, servants and retainers. Then he appointed his Vizier as his deputy and set out for his brother's dominions.

It so happened, however, that at midnight he remembered a

present which he had left at his palace. He returned for it unheralded, and entering his private chambers found his wife lying on a couch in the arms of a black slave. At this the world darkened before his eyes; and he thought: 'If this can happen when I am scarcely out of my city, how will this foul woman act when I am far away?' He then drew his sword and killed them both as they lay on the couch. Returning at once to his retainers, he gave orders for departure, and journeyed until he reached his brother's capital.

Shahriyar rejoiced at the news of his approach and went out to meet him. He embraced his guest and welcomed him to his festive city. But while Shahriyar sat entertaining his brother, Shahzaman, haunted by the thought of his wife's perfidy, was pale and sick at heart. Shahriyar perceived his distress, but said nothing, thinking that he might be troubled over the affairs of his kingdom. After a few days, however, Shahriyar said to him: 'I see that you are pale and care-worn.' Shahzaman answered: 'I am afflicted with a painful sore.' But he kept from him the story of his wife's treachery. Then Shahriyar invited his brother to go hunting with him, hoping that the sport might dispel his gloom. Shahzaman declined, and Shahriyar went alone to the hunt.

While Shahzaman sat at one of the windows overlooking the King's garden, he saw a door open in the palace, through which came twenty slave-girls and twenty Negroes. In their midst was his brother's queen, a woman of surpassing beauty. They made their way to the fountain, where they all undressed and sat on the grass. The King's wife then called out: 'Come Mass'ood!' and there promptly came to her a black slave, who mounted her after smothering her with embraces and kisses. So also did the Negroes with the slave-girls, revelling together till the approach of night.

When Shahzaman beheld this spectacle, he thought: 'By Allah, my misfortune is lighter than this!' He was dejected no longer, and ate and drank after his long abstinence.

Shahriyar, when he returned from the hunt, was surprised to see his brother restored to good spirits and full health. 'How is it, my brother,' asked Shahriyar, 'that when I last saw you, you were pale and melancholy, and now you look well and contented?'

'As for my melancholy,' replied Shahzaman, 'I shall now tell you the reason: but I cannot reveal the cause of my altered condition. Know then, that after I had received your invitation, I made preparations for the journey and left my city; but having forgotten the pearl which I was to present to you, I returned for it to the palace. There, on my couch, I found my wife lying in the embrace of a black slave. I killed them both and came to your kingdom, my mind oppressed with bitter thoughts.'

When he heard these words, Shahriyar urged him to tell the rest of his story. And so Shahzaman related to him all that he had seen in the King's garden that day.

Alarmed, but half in doubt, Shahriyar exclaimed: 'I will not believe that till I have seen it with my own eyes.'

'Then let it be given out,' suggested his brother, 'that you intend to go to the hunt again. Conceal yourself here with me, and you shall witness what I have seen.'

Upon this Shahriyar announced his intention to set forth on another expedition. The troops went out of the city with the tents, and King Shahriyar followed them. And after he had stayed a while in the camp, he gave orders to his slaves that no one was to be admitted to the King's tent. He then disguised himself and returned unnoticed to the palace, where his brother was waiting for him. They both sat at one of the windows overlooking the garden; and when they had been there a short time, the Queen and her women appeared with the black slaves, and behaved as Shahzaman had described.

Half demented at the sight, Shahriyar said to his brother: 'Let us renounce our royal state and roam the world until we find out if any other king has ever met with such disgrace.'

Shahzaman agreed to his proposal, and they went out in secret and travelled for many days and nights until they came to a meadow by the seashore. They refreshed themselves at a spring of water and sat down to rest under a tree.

Suddenly the waves of the sea surged and foamed before them, and there arose from the deep a black pillar which almost touched the sky. Struck with terror at the sight, they climbed into the tree. When they reached the top they were able to see that it was a jinnee of gigantic stature, carrying a chest on his head. The jinnee waded to the shore and walked towards the tree which sheltered the two brothers. Then, having seated himself beneath it, he opened the chest, and took from it a box, which he also opened; and there rose from the box a beautiful young girl, radiant as the sun.

'Chaste and honourable lady, whom I carried away on your wedding-night,' said the jinnee, 'I would sleep a little.' Then, laying his head upon her knees, the jinnee fell fast asleep.

Suddenly the girl lifted her head and saw the two Kings high in the tree. She laid the jinnee's head on the ground, and made signs to them which seemed to say: 'Come down, and have no fear of the jinnee.'

The two Kings pleaded with her to let them hide in safety, but the girl replied: 'If you do not come down, I will wake the jinnee, and he shall put you to a cruel death.'

They climbed down in fear, and at once she said: 'Come, pierce me with your rapiers.'

Shahriyar and Shahzaman faltered. But the girl repeated angrily: 'If you do not do my bidding, I will wake the jinnee.'

Afraid of the consequences, they proceeded to mount her in turn.

When they had remained with her as long as she desired, she took from her pocket a large purse, from which she drew ninety-eight rings threaded on a string. 'The owners of these,' she laughed triumphantly, 'have all enjoyed me under the very horn of this foolish jinnee. Therefore, give me your rings also.'

The two men gave her their rings.

'This jinnee,' she added, 'carried me away on my bridal night and imprisoned me in a box which he placed inside a chest. He fastened the chest with seven locks and deposited it at the bottom of the roaring sea. But he little knew how cunning we women are.'

The two Kings marvelled at her story, and said to each other: 'If such a thing could happen to a mighty jinnee, then our own misfortune is light indeed.' And they returned at once to the city.

As soon as they entered the palace, King Shahriyar put his wife to death, together with her women and the black slaves. Thenceforth he made it his custom to take a virgin in marriage to his bed each night, and kill her the next morning. This he continued to do for three years, until a clamour rose among the people, some of whom fled the country with their daughters.

At last came the day when the Vizier roamed the city in search of a virgin for the King, and could find none. Dreading the King's anger, he returned to his house with a heavy heart.

Now the Vizier had two daughters. The elder was called Shahrazad, and the younger Dunyazad. Shahrazad possessed many accomplishments and was versed in the wisdom of the poets and the legends of ancient kings.

That day Shahrazad noticed her father's anxiety and asked him what it was that troubled him. When the Vizier told her of his predicament, she said: 'Give me in marriage to this King: either I shall die and be a ransom for the daughters of Moslems, or live and be the cause of their deliverance.'

He earnestly pleaded with her against such a hazard; but Shahrazad was resolved, and would not yield to her father's entreaties.

'Beware,' said the Vizier, 'of the fate of the donkey in the fable:

The Fable of the Donkey, the Ox and the Farmer

'There was once a wealthy farmer who owned many herds of cattle. He knew the languages of beasts and birds. In one of his stalls he kept an ox and a donkey. At the end of each day, the ox came to the place where the donkey was tied and found it well swept and watered; the manger filled with sifted straw and well-winnowed barley; and the donkey lying at his ease (for his master seldom rode him).

'It chanced that one day the farmer heard the ox say to the donkey: "How fortunate you are! I am worn out with toil, while you rest here in comfort. You eat well-sifted barley and lack nothing. It is only occasionally that your master rides you. As for me, my life is perpetual drudgery at the plough and the millstone."

'The donkey answered: "When you go out into the field and the yoke is placed upon your neck, pretend to be ill and drop down on your belly. Do not rise even if they beat you; or if you do rise, lie down again. When they take you back and place the fodder before you, do not eat it. Abstain for a day or two; and thus shall you find a rest from toil."

'Remember that the farmer was there and heard what passed between them.

'And so when the ploughman came to the ox with his fodder, he ate scarcely any of it. And when the ploughman came the following morning to take him out into the field, the ox appeared to be far from well. Then the farmer said to the ploughman: "Take the donkey and use him at the plough all day!"

'The man returned, took the donkey in place of the ox, and drove him at the plough all day.

'When the day's work was done and the donkey returned to the stall, the ox thanked him for his good counsel. But the donkey made no reply and bitterly repented his rashness.

'Next day the ploughman came and took the donkey again

and made him labour till evening; so that when the donkey returned with his neck flayed by the yoke, and in a pitiful state of exhaustion, the ox again expressed his gratitude to him, and praised his sagacity.

'"If only I had kept my wisdom to myself!" thought the donkey. Then, turning to the ox, he said: "I have just heard my master say to his servant: 'If the ox does not recover soon, take him to the slaughterhouse and dispose of him.' My anxiety for your safety prompts me, my friend, to let you know of this before it is too late. And peace be with you!"

'When he heard the donkey's words, the ox thanked him and said: "Tomorrow I will go to work freely and willingly." He ate all his fodder and even licked the manger clean.

'Early next morning the farmer, accompanied by his wife, went to visit the ox in his stall. The ploughman came and led out the ox, who, at the sight of his master, broke wind and frisked about in all directions. And the farmer laughed so, he fell over on his back.'

When she heard her father's story, Shahrazad said: 'Nothing will shake my faith in the mission I am destined to fulfil.'

So the Vizier arrayed his daughter in bridal garments and decked her with jewels and made ready to announce Shahrazad's wedding to the King.

Before saying farewell to her sister, Shahrazad gave her these instructions: 'When I am received by the King, I shall send for you. Then, when the King has finished his act with me, you must say: "Tell me, my sister, some tale of marvel to beguile the night." Then I will tell you a tale which, if Allah wills, shall be the means of our deliverance.'

The Vizier went with his daughter to the King. And when the King had taken the maiden Shahrazad to his chamber and had lain with her, she wept and said: 'I have a young sister to whom I wish to bid farewell.'

The King sent for Dunyazad. When she arrived, she threw her arms round her sister's neck, and seated herself by her side.

Then Dunyazad said to Shahrazad: 'Tell us, my sister, a tale of marvel, so that the night may pass pleasantly.'

'Gladly,' she answered, 'if the King permits.'

And the King, who was troubled with sleeplessness, eagerly listened to the tale of Shahrazad . . .

NICCOLÒ MACHIAVELLI

from *The Prince*

XV
The things for which men, and especially princes, are praised or blamed

It now remains for us to see how a prince must regulate his conduct towards his subjects or his allies. I know that this has often been written about before, and so I hope it will not be thought presumptuous for me to do so, as, especially in discussing this subject, I draw up an original set of rules. But since my intention is to say something that will prove of practical use to the inquirer, I have thought it proper to represent things as they are in a real truth, rather than as they are imagined. Many have dreamed up republics and principalities which have never in truth been known to exist; the gulf between how one should live and how one does live is so wide that a man who neglects what is actually done for what should be done moves towards self-destruction rather than self-preservation. The fact is that a man who wants to act virtuously in every way necessarily comes to grief among so many who are not virtuous. Therefore if a prince wants to maintain his rule he must be prepared not to be virtuous, and to make use of this or not according to need.

So leaving aside imaginary things about a prince, and referring only to those which truly exist, I say that whenever men are discussed and especially princes (who are more exposed to view), they are judged for various qualities which earn them either praise or condemnation. Some, for example, are held to be generous, and others miserly (I use the Tuscan word rather than the word avaricious: we also call a man who is mean with what he possesses, miserly, whereas avaricious applies also to a man who wants to plunder others). Some are held to be benefactors, others are called grasping; some cruel, some compassionate; one man faithless, another faithful; one man effeminate and cowardly, another fierce and courageous; one man courteous, another proud; one man lascivious, another chaste; one guileless, another crafty; one stubborn, another flexible; one grave, another frivolous; one religious, another sceptical; and so forth. I know everyone will agree that it would be most laudable if a prince possessed all the qualities deemed to be good among those I have enumerated. But, because of conditions in the world, princes cannot have those qualities, or observe them completely. So a prince has of necessity to be so prudent that he knows how to escape the evil reputation attached to those vices which could lose him his state, and how to avoid those vices which are not so dangerous, if he possibly can; but, if he cannot, he need not worry so much about the latter. And then, he must not flinch from being blamed for vices which are necessary for safeguarding the state. This is because, taking everything into account, he will find that some of the things that appear to be virtues will, if he practises them, ruin him, and some of the things that appear to be vices will bring him security and prosperity.

XVI
Generosity and parsimony

So, starting with the first of the qualities I enumerated above, I say it would be splendid if one had a reputation for generosity; none the less if you do in fact earn a reputation for generosity you will come to grief. This is because if your generosity is good and sincere it may pass unnoticed and it will not save you from being reproached for its opposite. If you want to sustain a reputation for generosity, therefore, you have to be ostentatiously lavish; and a prince acting in that fashion will soon squander all his resources, only to be forced in the end, if he wants to maintain his reputation, to lay excessive burdens on the people, to impose extortionate taxes, and to do everything else he can to raise money. This will start to make his subjects hate him, and, since he will have impoverished himself, he will be generally despised. As a result, because of this generosity of his, having injured many and rewarded few, he will be vulnerable to the first minor setback, and the first real danger he encounters will bring him to grief. When he realizes this and tries to retrace his path he will immediately be reputed a miser.

So because a prince cannot practise the virtue of generosity in such a way that he is noted for it, except to his cost, he should if he is prudent not mind being called a miser. In time he will be recognized as being essentially a generous man, seeing that because of his parsimony his existing revenues are enough for him, he can defend himself against an aggressor, and he can embark on campaigns without burdening the people. So he proves himself generous to all those from whom he takes nothing, and they are innumerable, and miserly towards all those to whom he gives nothing, and they are few. In our own times great things have been accomplished only by those who have been held miserly, and the others have met disaster. Pope Julius II made use of a reputation for generosity to win the papacy but subsequently he made no effort to maintain this reputation, because he wanted to be able to finance his wars. The present king of France has been able to wage so many wars without taxing his subjects excessively only because his long-standing parsimony enabled him to meet the additional expenses involved. Were the present king of Spain renowned for his generosity he would not have started and successfully concluded so many enterprises.

So a prince must think little of it, if he incurs the name of miser, so as not to rob his subjects, to be able to defend himself, not to become poor and despicable, not to be forced to grow rapacious. Miserliness is one of those vices which sustain his rule. Someone may object: Caesar came to power by virtue of his generosity, and many others, because they practised and were known for their generosity, have risen to the very highest positions. My answer to this is as follows. Either you are already a prince, or you are on the way to becoming one. In the first case, your generosity will be to your cost; in the second, it is certainly necessary to have a reputation for generosity. Caesar was one of those who wanted to establish his own rule over Rome; but if, after he had established it, he had remained alive and not moderated his expenditure he would have fallen from power.

Again, someone may retort: there have been many princes who have won great successes with their armies, and who have had the reputation of being extremely generous. My reply to this is: the prince gives away what is his own or his subjects', or else what belongs to others. In the first case he should be frugal; in the second, he should indulge his generosity to the full. The prince who campaigns with his armies, who lives by pillaging, sacking and extortion, disposes of what belongs to aliens; and he must be open-handed, otherwise the soldiers would refuse to follow him. And you can be more liberal with what does not belong to you or your subjects, as Caesar, Cyrus and Alexander were. Giving away what belongs to strangers in no way affects your standing at home; rather it increases it. You hurt yourself only when you give away what is your own. There is nothing so self-defeating as generosity: in the act of practising it, you lose the ability to do so, and you become either poor and despised or, seeking to escape poverty, rapacious and hated. A prince must try to avoid, above all else, being despised and hated; and generosity results in your being both. Therefore it is wiser to incur the reputation of being a miser, which brings forth ignominy but not hatred, than to be forced by seeking a name for generosity to incur a reputation for rapacity, which brings you hatred as well as ignominy.

XVII
Cruelty and compassion; and whether it is better to be loved than feared, or the reverse

Taking others of the qualities I enumerated above, I say that a prince must want to have a reputation for compassion rather than for cruelty: none the less, he must be careful that he does not make bad use of compassion. Cesare Borgia was accounted cruel; nevertheless, this cruelty of his reformed the Romagna, brought it unity, and restored order and obedience. On reflection, it will be seen that there was more compassion in Cesare than in the Florentine people, who, to escape being called cruel, allowed Pistoia to be devastated. So a prince must not worry if he incurs reproach for his cruelty so long as he keeps his subjects united and loyal. By making an example or two he will prove more compassionate than those who, being too compassionate, allow disorders which lead to murder and rapine. These nearly always harm the whole community, whereas executions ordered by a prince only affect individuals. A new prince, of all rulers, finds it impossible to avoid a reputation for cruelty, because of the abundant dangers inherent in a newly won state. Vergil, through the mouth of Dido, says:

> Res dura, et regni novitas me talia cogunt
> Moliri, et late fines custode tueri.

None the less, a prince must be slow to believe allegations and to take action, and must watch that he does not come to be afraid of his own shadow; his behaviour must be tempered by humanity and prudence so that over-confidence does not make him rash or excessive distrust make him unbearable.

From this arises the following question: whether it is better to be loved than feared, or the reverse. The answer is that one would like to be both the one and the other; but because it is difficult to combine them, it is far better to be feared than loved if you cannot be both. One can make this generalization about men: they are ungrateful, fickle, liars, and deceivers, they shun danger and are greedy for profit; while you treat them well, they are yours. They would shed their blood for you, risk their property, their lives, their sons, so long, as I said above, as danger is remote; but when you are in danger they turn away. Any prince who has come to depend entirely on promises and has taken no other precautions ensures his own ruin; friendship which is bought with money and not with greatness and nobility of mind is paid for, but it does not last and it yields nothing. Men worry less about doing an injury to one who makes himself loved than to one who makes himself feared. For love is secured by a bond of gratitude which men, wretched creatures that they are, break when it is to their advantage to do so; but fear is strengthened by a dread of punishment which is always effective.

The prince must none the less make himself feared in such a way that, if he is not loved, at least he escapes being hated. For fear is quite compatible with an absence of hatred; and the prince can always avoid hatred if he abstains from the property of his subjects and citizens and from their women. If, even so, it proves necessary to execute someone, this is to be done only when there is proper justification and manifest reason for it. But above all a prince must abstain from the property of others; because men sooner forget the death of their father than the loss of their patrimony. It is always possible to find pretexts for confiscating someone's property; and a prince who starts to live by rapine always finds pretexts for seizing what belongs to others. On the other hand, pretexts for executing someone are harder to find and they are sooner gone.

However, when a prince is campaigning with his soldiers and is in command of a large army then he need not worry about having a reputation for cruelty; because, without such a reputation, no army was ever kept united and disciplined. Among the admirable achievements of Hannibal is included this: that although he led a huge army, made up of countless different races, on foreign campaigns, there was never any dissension, either among the troops themselves or against their leader, whether things were going well or badly. For this, his inhuman cruelty was wholly responsible. It was this, along with his countless other qualities, which made him feared and respected by his soldiers. If it had not been for his cruelty, his other qualities would not have been enough. The historians, having given little thought to this, on the one hand admire what Hannibal achieved, and on the other condemn what made his achievements possible.

That his other qualities would not have been enough by themselves can be proved by looking at Scipio, a man unique in his own time and through all recorded history. His armies mutinied against him in Spain, and the only reason for this was his excessive leniency, which allowed his soldiers more licence than was good for military discipline. Fabius Maximus reproached him for this in the Senate and called him a corrupter of the Roman legions. Again, when the Locrians were plundered by one of Scipio's officers, he neither gave them satisfaction nor punished his officer's insubordination; and this was all because of his being too lenient by nature. By way of excuse for him some senators argued that many men were better at not making mistakes themselves than at correcting them in others. But in time Scipio's lenient nature would have spoilt his fame and glory had he continued to indulge it during his command; when he lived under orders from the Senate, however, this fatal characteristic of his was not only concealed but even brought him glory.

So, on this question of being loved or feared, I conclude that since some men love as they please but fear when the prince pleases, a wise prince should rely on what he controls, not on what he cannot control. He must only endeavour, as I said, to escape being hated.

XVIII
How princes should honour their word

Everyone realizes how praiseworthy it is for a prince to honour his word and to be straightforward rather than crafty in his dealings; none the less contemporary experience shows that princes who have achieved great things have been those who have given their word lightly, who have known how to trick men with their cunning, and who, in the end, have overcome those abiding by honest principles.

You must understand, therefore, that there are two ways of fighting: by law or by force. The first way is natural to men, and the second to beasts. But as the first way often proves inadequate one must needs have recourse to the second. So a prince must understand how to make a nice use of the beast and the man. The ancient writers taught princes about this by an allegory, when they described how Achilles and many other princes of the ancient world were sent to be brought up by Chiron, the centaur, so that he might train them his way. All the allegory means, in making the teacher half beast and half man, is that a prince must know how to act according to the nature of both, and that he cannot survive otherwise.

So, as a prince is forced to know how to act like a beast, he must learn from the fox and the lion; because the lion is defenceless against traps and a fox is defenceless against wolves. Therefore one must be a fox in order to recognize traps, and a lion to frighten off wolves. Those who simply act like lions are stupid. So it follows that a prudent ruler cannot, and must not, honour his word when it places him at a disadvantage and when the reasons for which he made his promise no longer exist. If all men were good, this precept would not be good; but because men are wretched creatures who would not keep their word to you, you need not keep your word to them. And no prince ever lacked good excuses to colour his bad faith. One could give innumerable modern instances of this, showing how many pacts and promises have been made null and void by the bad faith of princes: those who have known best how to imitate the fox have come off best. But one must know how to colour one's actions and to be a great liar and deceiver. Men are so simple, and so much creatures of circumstance, that the deceiver will always find someone ready to be deceived.

There is one fresh example I do not want to omit. Alexander VI never did anything, or thought of anything, other than deceiving men; and he always found victims for his deceptions. There never was a man capable of such convincing asseverations, or so ready to swear to the truth of something, who would honour his word less. None the less his deceptions always had the result he intended, because he was a past master in the art.

A prince, therefore, need not necessarily have all the good qualities I mentioned above, but he should certainly appear to have them. I would even go so far as to say that if he has these qualities and always behaves accordingly he will find them harmful; if he only appears to have them they will render him service. He should appear to be compassionate, faithful to his word, kind, guileless and devout. And indeed he should be so. But his disposition should be such that, if he needs to be the opposite, he knows how. You must realize this: that a prince, and especially a new prince, cannot observe all those things which give men a reputation for virtue, because in order to maintain his state he is often forced to act in defiance of good faith, of charity, of kindness, of religion. And so he should have a flexible disposition, varying as fortune and circumstances dictate. As I said above, he should not deviate from what is good, if that is possible, but he should know how to do evil, if that is necessary.

A prince, then, must be very careful not to say a word which does not seem inspired by the five qualities I mentioned earlier. To those seeing and hearing him, he should appear a man of compassion, a man of good faith, a man of integrity, a kind and a religious man. And there is nothing so important as to seem to have this last quality. Men in general judge by their eyes rather than by their hands; because everyone is in a position to watch, few are in a position to come in close touch with you. Everyone sees what you appear to be, few experience what you really are. And those few dare not gainsay the many who are backed by the majesty of the state. In the actions of all men, and especially of princes, where there is no court of appeal, one judges by the result. So let a prince set about the task of conquering, and maintaining his state; his methods will always be judged honourable and will be universally praised. The common people are always impressed by appearances and results. In this context, there are only common people, and there is no leeway for the few when the many are firmly sustained. A certain contemporary ruler, whom it is better not to name, never preaches anything except peace and good faith; and he is an enemy of both one and the other, and if he had ever honoured either of them he would have lost either his standing or his state many times over.

XIX
The need to avoid contempt and hatred

Now, having talked about the most important of the qualities enumerated above, I want to discuss the others briefly under this generalization: that the prince should, as I have already suggested, determine to avoid anything which will make him hated and despised. So long as he does so, he will have done what he should and he will run no risk whatsoever if he is reproached for the other vices I mentioned. He will be hated above all if, as I said, he is rapacious and aggressive with regard to the property and the women of his subjects. He must refrain from these. As long as he does not rob the great majority of their property or their honour, they remain content. He then has to contend only with the ambition of a few, and that can be dealt with easily and in a variety of ways. He will be despised if he has a reputation for being fickle, frivolous, effeminate, cowardly, irresolute; a prince should avoid this like the plague and strive to demonstrate in his actions grandeur, courage, sobriety, strength. When settling disputes between his subjects, he should ensure that his judgement is irrevocable; and he should be so regarded that no one ever dreams of trying to deceive or trick him.

The prince who succeeds in having himself thus regarded is highly esteemed; and against a man who is highly esteemed conspiracy is difficult, and open attack is difficult, provided he is recognized as a great man, who is respected by his subjects. There are two things a prince must fear: internal subversion from his subjects; and external aggression by foreign powers. Against the latter, his defence lies in being well armed and having good allies; and if he is well armed he will always have good allies. In addition, domestic affairs will always remain under control provided that relations with external powers are under control and if indeed they were not disturbed by a conspiracy. Even if there is disturbance abroad, if the prince has ordered his government and lived as I said, and if he does not capitulate, he will always repulse every onslaught, just as I said Nabis the Spartan did. Now, as far as his subjects are concerned, when there is no disturbance abroad the prince's chief fear must be a secret conspiracy. He can adequately guard against this if he avoids being hated or scorned and keeps the people satisfied: this, as I have said above at length, is crucial. One of the most powerful safeguards a prince can have against conspiracies is to avoid being hated by the populace. This is because the conspirator always thinks that by killing the prince he will satisfy the people; but if he thinks that he will outrage the people, he will never have the courage to go ahead with his enterprise, because there are countless obstacles in the path of a conspirator. As experience shows, there have been many conspiracies but few of them have achieved their end. This is because the conspirator needs others to help him, and those have to be men who, he believes, are disgruntled. But as soon as he reveals his mind to a man who is dissatisfied he gives him the means to get satisfaction, because by telling all he knows the latter can hope to obtain all he wants. Seeing the sure profit to be won by informing, and the highly dangerous and doubtful alternative, a man must be either a rare friend indeed or else an utterly relentless enemy of the prince to keep faith with you. To put it briefly, I say that on the side of the conspirator there is nothing except fear, envy, and the terrifying prospect of punishment; on the side of the prince there is the majesty of government, there are laws, the resources of his friends and of the state to protect him. Add to all these the goodwill of the people, and it is unthinkable that anyone should be so rash as to conspire. For whereas in the normal course of events a conspirator has cause for fear before he acts, in this case he has cause for fear afterwards as well, seeing that the people are hostile to him. He will have accomplished his crime, and, because the people are against him, he will have no place of refuge.

I could give countless illustrations of this; but I will content myself with just one, which happened in the time of our fathers. The Canneschi conspired against and killed messer Annibale Bentivogli, grandfather of the present Annibale, and prince of Bologna. There remained as his heir only messer Giovanni, who was still in swaddling clothes. Immediately this murder was perpetrated, the people rose up and killed all the Canneschi. They were inspired by the goodwill that existed for the House of Bentivoglio at that period. It was so great that, although there was no member of the family left in Bologna to take over the government on the death of Annibale, the citizens of Bologna, hearing that there was someone in Florence who was of the Bentivoglio family but had until then been thought to be the son of a smith, went there to find him. They entrusted him with the government of the city; and he ruled until Giovanni was old enough to assume the government himself.

I conclude, therefore, that when a prince has the goodwill of the people he must not worry about conspiracies; but when the people are hostile and regard him with hatred he must go in fear of everything and everyone. Well-organized states and wise princes have always taken great pains not to make the nobles despair, and to satisfy the people and keep them content; this is one of the most important tasks a prince must undertake.

Among kingdoms which are well organized and governed, in our own time, is that of France: it possesses countless valuable institutions, on which the king's freedom of action and security depend. The first of these is the parliament and its authority. For the lawgiver of the French kingdom, knowing the ambition and insolence of the powerful, judged it necessary that they should be restrained by having a bit in their mouths. On the other hand, he wanted to protect the masses, knowing how they feared, and therefore hated, the nobles. He did not want this to be the particular responsibility of the king, because he wished to save him from being reproached by the nobles for favouring the people and by the people for favouring the nobles. So he instituted an independent arbiter to crush the nobles and favour the weak, without bringing reproach on the king. There could be no better or more sensible institution, nor one more effective in ensuring the security of the king and the kingdom.

From this can be drawn another noteworthy consideration: that princes should delegate to others the enactment of unpopular measures and keep in their own hands the means of winning favours. Again, I conclude that a prince should value the nobles, but not make himself hated by the people.

Many who have studied the lives and deaths of certain Roman emperors may perhaps believe that they provide examples contradicting my opinion; some emperors who led consistently worthy lives, and showed strength of character, none the less fell from power, or were even done to death by their own men who conspired against them. As I wish to answer these objections, I shall discuss the characters of some of the emperors, showing that the reasons for their downfall are not different from those I have adduced. I shall submit for consideration examples which are well known to students of the period. I shall also restrict myself to all those emperors who came to power from Marcus the philosopher to Maximinus. These were: Marcus Aurelius, Commodus his son, Pertinax, Julian, Severus, Caracalla his son, Macrinus, Heliogabalus, Alexander and Maximinus.

First, it is to be noted that whereas other princes have to contend only with the ambition of the nobles and the insolence of the people, the Roman emperors encountered a third difficulty: they had to contend with the cruelty and avarice of the soldiers. This was a hard task and it was responsible for the downfall of many, since it was difficult to satisfy both the soldiers and the populace. The latter, being peace-loving, liked unadventurous emperors, while the soldiers loved a warlike ruler, and one who was arrogant, cruel and rapacious. They wanted him to treat the people accordingly, so that they could be paid more and could give vent to their own avarice and cruelty. As a result, those emperors who did not have the natural authority or the standing to hold both the soldiers and the populace in check always came to grief. Most of them, especially those who were new to government, when they recognized the difficulty of satisfying these two diverse elements, appeased the soldiers and did not worry about injuring the populace. This policy was necessary: princes cannot help arousing hatred in some quarters, so first they must strive not to be hated by all and every class of subject; and when this proves impossible, they should strive assiduously to escape the hatred of the most powerful classes. Therefore those emperors who, because they were new men, needed out of the ordinary support, were more ready to throw in their lot with the soldiers than with the people. None the less, this proved to be advantageous or not depending on whether the ruler knew how to maintain his standing with the troops. Now, for the reasons given above, it came about that Marcus Aurelius, Pertinax and Alexander, who all lived unadventurously, who loved justice, hated cruelty, were kind and courteous, all, Marcus apart, had an unhappy end. Marcus alone was held during his life and after in high esteem, because he succeeded to the empire by hereditary right, and did not have to thank either the soldiers or the populace for it. Then, as he possessed many qualities which earned him great respect, all his life he succeeded in holding both of these in check and he was never hated or scorned. But Pertinax came to grief in the early stages of his administration; he was created emperor against the will of the soldiers, who had been used to living licentiously under Commodus and so could not tolerate the decency which Pertinax wished to impose on them. So the emperor made himself hated, and also, since he was an old man, scorned.

And here it should be noted that one can be hated just as much for good deeds as for evil ones; therefore, as I said above, a prince who wants to maintain his rule is often forced not to be good, because whenever that class of men on which you believe your continued rule depends is corrupt, whether it be the populace, or soldiers, or nobles, you have to satisfy it by adopting the same disposition; and then good deeds are your enemies. But let us come to Alexander. He was a man of such goodness that, among the other things for which he is given credit, it is said that during the fourteen years he reigned he never put anyone to death without trial. None the less, as he was thought effeminate, and a man who let himself be ruled by his mother, he came to be scorned, and the army conspired against him and killed him.

Discussing in contrast the characters of Commodus, Severus, Antoninus Caracalla and Maximinus, you will find them to have been extremely cruel and rapacious. To satisfy the soldiers, there was no kind of injury they did not inflict on the people; and all of them, except Severus, came to an unhappy end. Severus was a man of such prowess that, keeping the soldiers friendly, even though the people were oppressed by him, he reigned successfully to the end; this was because his prowess so impressed the soldiers and the people that the latter were in a certain manner left astonished and stupefied and the former stayed respectful and content.

Because what Severus did was remarkable and outstanding for a new prince, I want to show briefly how well he knew how to act the part of both a fox and a lion, whose natures, as I say above, must be imitated by a new prince. Knowing the indolence of the emperor Julian, Severus persuaded the troops he commanded in Slavonia to march on Rome to avenge the death of Pertinax, who had been put to death by the Praetorian Guards. Under this pretext, without any indication that he aspired to the empire, he moved the army against Rome; and he arrived in Italy before it was known that he had set out. When he came, the Senate, out of fear, elected him emperor and put Julian to death. After this start, there remained two obstacles in the way of his becoming master of all the state: one was in Asia, where Pescennius Niger, commander of the Asiatic army, had had himself proclaimed emperor; the other was in the west, where Albinus also aspired to the empire. Judging it was dangerous to show himself hostile to both of them, Severus decided to attack Niger and to trick Albinus. He wrote to the latter saying that, having been elected emperor by the Senate, he wished to share the high rank with him; he sent him the title of Caesar and, through a resolution in the Senate, he made him co-emperor. Albinus took all these things at their face value. But once Severus had defeated Niger and put him to death, and had pacified the East, he returned to Rome and complained in the Senate that Albinus, not recognizing the favours he had received from him, had treacherously sought to kill him. Because of this, Severus added, it was necessary for him to go and punish such ingratitude. He then marched against him in France, and took from him his state and his life.

So whoever carefully studies what this man did will find that he had the qualities of a ferocious lion and a very cunning fox, and that he was feared and respected by everyone, yet not hated by the troops. And it will not be thought anything to marvel at if Severus, an upstart, proved himself able to maintain such great power; because his tremendous prestige always protected him from the hatred which his plundering had inspired in the people. Now Antoninus Caracalla, his son, was also a man of splendid qualities which astonished the people and endeared him to the soldiers; he was a military man, capable of any exertion, and he scorned softness of any kind, at the table or elsewhere. This won him the devotion of the troops. None the less, his ferocity and cruelty were so great and unparalleled (after countless individual murders, he put to death great numbers of Romans and all the citizens of Alexandria) that he became universally hated. Even those closest to him started to fear him; and as a result he was killed by a centurion, when he was surrounded by his troops. Here it should be noted that princes cannot escape death if the attempt is made by a fanatic, because anyone who has no fear of death himself can succeed in inflicting it; on the other hand, there is less need for a prince to be afraid, since such assassinations are very rare. However, the prince should restrain himself from inflicting grave injury on anyone in his service whom he has close to him in his affairs of state. That was how Antoninus erred. He put to death, with disgrace, a brother of that centurion, whom in turn he threatened every day even though still retaining him in his bodyguard. This rash behaviour was calculated to bring him grief, as in the end it did.

But let us come to Commodus, for whom ruling the empire

was an easy task, since being the son of Marcus Aurelius he held it by hereditary right. He had only to follow in the footsteps of his father, and then he would have satisfied the soldiers and the people. But, as he was of a cruel, bestial disposition, he endeavoured to indulge the soldiers and make them dissolute, in order to exercise his rapacity on the people. On the other hand, he forgot his dignity, often descended into the amphitheatres to fight with the gladiators, and did other ignoble things hardly worthy of the imperial majesty; as a result the soldiers came to despise him. So, being hated on the one side and scorned on the other, he fell victim to a conspiracy which ended in his death.

It now remains for us to describe the character of Maximinus. He was a very warlike man, and the troops, being sick of the effeminacies of Alexander, whom I discussed above, elected him emperor after Alexander's death. He did not hold the empire for long, because two things made him hated and despised: first, he was of the lowest origins, having once been a shepherd in Thrace (this was well known to everybody and lowered him in everyone's eyes); second, at his accession he put off going to Rome to be formally hailed as emperor, and he impressed people as being extremely savage because he inflicted many cruelties through his prefects in Rome and in other parts of the empire. As a result, there was a universal upsurge of indignation against him because of his mean birth, and an upsurge of hatred caused by fear of his ferocity. First Africa rebelled, and then the Senate with the support of all the people of Rome. All Italy conspired against him. The conspiracy was joined by his own troops who, when they were besieging Aquileia and finding difficulties in taking the town, sickened of his cruelty; seeing how many enemies he had they feared him less, and they killed him.

I do not want to discuss Heliogabalus, or Macrinus, or Julian, who were thoroughly despised and therefore did not last long. Instead I shall conclude by saying that contemporary princes are less troubled by this problem of having to take extraordinary measures to satisfy the soldiers. They do have to give them some consideration; but notwithstanding this the problem is soon settled, because princes today do not possess standing armies which, like the armies of the Roman Empire, have become firmly established in the government and administration of conquered territories. So if in Roman times it was necessary to satisfy the demands of the soldiers rather than those of the people, this was because the soldiers had more power than the people. In our own times it is necessary for all rulers, except the Turk and the Sultan, to conciliate the people rather than the soldiers, because the people are the more powerful. I make an exception of the Turk, because that ruler maintains a standing army of twelve thousand infantry and fifteen thousand cavalry, essential to the security and strength of his kingdom; and so he must subordinate every other consideration to that of retaining their loyalty. Similarly, the Sultan's dominion is completely in the hands of his soldiers, and he also, without regard for the people, must make sure of their allegiance to him. You should note that the Sultan's state differs from all the other principalities, being similar to the papacy, which cannot be called either a hereditary or a new principality. It is not the sons of the former ruler who inherit and become rulers but the one elected by those with the authority to do so. As this system is an ancient one it cannot be classified among the new principalities. There are none of the difficulties encountered in a new principality; although the prince is new, the institutions of the state are old, and they are devised to accommodate him as if he were the hereditary ruler.

But let us go back to the subject. I say that whoever follows my argument will realize that the downfall of the emperors I mentioned was caused by either hatred or scorn. He will also recognize why it happened that, some of them behaving one way and some of them another, in both cases one ended happily and the rest came to grief. As they were new princes, it was useless and disastrous for Pertinax and Alexander to want to imitate

Marcus Aurelius, who succeeded by hereditary right; similarly it was fatal for Caracalla, Commodus and Maximinus to imitate Severus, since they lacked the prowess to follow in his footsteps. Therefore, a new prince in a new principality cannot imitate the actions of Marcus Aurelius, nor is he bound to follow those of Severus. Rather, he should select from Severus the qualities necessary to establish his state, and from Marcus Aurelius those which are conducive to its maintenance and glory after it has been stabilized and made secure.

LEWIS CARROLL

from *Through the Looking-Glass*

CHAPTER I
Looking-Glass House

One thing was certain, that the *white* kitten had nothing to do
with it – it was the black kitten's fault entirely. For the white
kitten had been having its face washed by the old cat for the last
quarter of an hour (and bearing it pretty well, considering): so
you see that it *couldn't* have had any hand in the mischief.

The way Dinah washed her children's faces was this: first she
held the poor thing down by its ear with one paw, and then with
the other paw she rubbed its face all over, the wrong way, beginning at the nose: and just now, as I said, she was hard at work on
the white kitten, which was lying quite still and trying to purr
– no doubt feeling that it was all meant for its good.

But the black kitten had been finished with earlier in the afternoon, and so, while Alice was sitting curled up in a corner of the
great arm-chair, half talking to herself and half asleep, the kitten
had been having a grand game of romps with the ball of worsted
Alice had been trying to wind up, and had been rolling it up and
down till it had all come undone again; and there it was, spread
over the hearth-rug, all knots and tangles, with the kitten running
after its own tail in the middle.

'Oh, you wicked wicked little thing!' cried Alice, catching up
the kitten, and giving it a little kiss to make it understand that it
was in disgrace. 'Really, Dinah ought to have taught you better

manners! You *ought*, Dinah, you know you ought!' she added, looking reproachfully at the old cat, and speaking in as cross a voice as she could manage – and then she scrambled back into the arm-chair, taking the kitten and the worsted with her, and began winding up the ball again. But she didn't get on very fast, as she was talking all the time, sometimes to the kitten, and some-times to herself. Kitty sat very demurely on her knee, pretending to watch the progress of the winding, and now and then putting out one paw and gently touching the ball, as if it would be glad to help if it might.

'Do you know what to-morrow is, Kitty?' Alice began. 'You'd have guessed if you'd been up in the window with me – only Dinah was making you tidy, so you couldn't. I was watching the boys getting in sticks for the bonfire – and it wants plenty of sticks, Kitty! Only it got so cold, and it snowed so, they had to leave off. Never mind, Kitty, we'll go and see the bonfire to-morrow.' Here Alice wound two or three turns of the worsted round the kitten's neck, just to see how it would look: this led to a scramble, in which the ball rolled down upon the floor, and yards and yards of it got unwound again.

'Do you know, I was so angry, Kitty,' Alice went on, as soon as they were comfortably settled again, 'when I saw all the mischief you had been doing, I was very nearly opening the window, and putting you out into the snow! And you'd have deserved it, you little mischievous darling! What have you got to say for yourself? Now don't interrupt me!' she went on, hold-ing up one finger. 'I'm going to tell you all your faults. Number one: you squeaked twice while Dinah was washing your face this morning. Now you can't deny it, Kitty: I heard you! What's that you say?' (pretending that the kitten was speaking). 'Her paw went into your eye? Well, that's *your* fault, for keeping your eyes open – if you'd shut them tight up, it wouldn't have happened. Now don't make any more excuses, but listen! Number two: you pulled Snowdrop away by the tail just as I had put down the saucer of milk before her! What, you were thirsty, were you? How do you know she wasn't thirsty too? Now for number three: you unwound every bit of the worsted while I wasn't looking!

'That's three faults, Kitty, and you've not been punished for any of them yet. You know I'm saving up all your punishments for Wednesday week – Suppose they had saved up all *my* punishments?' she went on, talking more to herself than the kitten. 'What *would* they do at the end of a year? I should be sent to prison, I suppose, when the day came. Or – let me see – suppose each punishment was to be going without a dinner: then, when the miserable day came, I should have to go without fifty dinners at once! Well, I shouldn't mind *that* much! I'd far rather go without them than eat them!

'Do you hear the snow against the window-panes, Kitty? How nice and soft it sounds! Just as if some one was kissing the window all over outside. I wonder if the snow *loves* the trees and fields, that it kisses them so gently? And then it covers them up snug, you know, with a white quilt; and perhaps it says "Go to sleep, darlings, till the summer comes again." And when they wake up in the summer, Kitty, they dress themselves all in green, and dance about – whenever the wind blows – oh, that's very pretty!' cried Alice, dropping the ball of worsted to clap her hands. 'And I do so *wish* it was true! I'm sure the woods look sleepy in the autumn, when the leaves are getting brown.

'Kitty, can you play chess? Now, don't smile, my dear, I'm asking it seriously. Because, when we were playing just now, you watched just as if you understood it: and when I said "Check!" you purred! Well, it *was* a nice check, Kitty, and really I might have won, if it hadn't been for that nasty Knight, that came wriggling down among my pieces. Kitty, dear, let's pretend . . .' And here I wish I could tell you half the things Alice used to say, beginning with her favourite phrase 'Let's pretend.' She had had quite a long argument with her sister only the day before – all because Alice had begun with 'Let's pretend we're kings and queens;' and her sister, who liked being very exact, had argued that they couldn't, because there were only two of them, and Alice had been reduced at last to say 'Well *you* can be one of them, then, and *I'll* be all the rest.' And once she had really frightened her old nurse by shouting suddenly in her ear, 'Nurse! Do let's pretend that I'm a hungry hyæna, and you're a bone!'

But this is taking us away from Alice's speech to the kitten. 'Let's pretend that you're the Red Queen, Kitty! Do you know, I think if you sat up and folded your arms, you'd look exactly like her. Now do try, there's a dear!' And Alice got the Red Queen off the table, and set it up before the kitten as a model for it to imitate: however, the thing didn't succeed, principally, Alice said, because the kitten wouldn't fold its arms properly. So, to punish it, she held it up to the Looking-glass, that it might see how sulky it was, '– and if you're not good directly,' she added, 'I'll put you through into Looking-glass House. How would you like *that*?

'Now, if you'll only attend, Kitty, and not talk so much, I'll tell you all my ideas about Looking-glass House. First, there's the room you can see through the glass – that's just the same as our drawing-room, only the things go the other way. I can see all of it when I get upon a chair – all but the bit just behind the fireplace. Oh! I do so wish I could see *that* bit! I want so much to know whether they've a fire in the winter: you never *can* tell, you know, unless our fire smokes, and then smoke comes up in that room too – but that may be only pretence, just to make it look as if they had a fire. Well then, the books are something like our books, only the words go the wrong way: I know *that*, because I've held up one of our books to the glass, and then they hold up one in the other room.

'How would you like to live in Looking-glass House, Kitty? I wonder if they'd give you milk in there? Perhaps Looking-glass milk isn't good to drink – but oh, Kitty! now we come to the passage. You can just see a little *peep* of the passage in Looking-glass House, if you leave the door of our drawing-room wide open: and it's very like our passage as far as you can see, only you know it may be quite different on beyond. Oh, Kitty, how nice it would be if we could only get through into Looking-glass House! I'm sure it's got, oh! such beautiful things in it! Let's pretend there's a way of getting through into it, somehow, Kitty. Let's pretend the glass has got all soft like gauze, so that we can get through. Why, it's turning into a sort of mist now, I declare! It'll be easy enough to get through . . .' She was up on the chimney-piece while she said this, though she hardly knew how she had got there. And certainly the glass *was* beginning to melt away, just like a bright silvery mist.

In another moment Alice was through the glass, and had jumped lightly down into the Looking-glass room. The very first thing she did was to look whether there was a fire in the fireplace, and she was quite pleased to find that there was a real one, blazing away as brightly as the one she had left behind. 'So I shall be as warm here as I was in the old room,' thought Alice: 'warmer, in fact, because there'll be no one here to scold me away from the fire. Oh, what fun it'll be, when they see me through the glass in here, and ca'n't get at me!'

Then she began looking about, and noticed that what could be seen from the old room was quite common and uninteresting, but that all the rest was as different as possible. For instance, the pictures on the wall next the fire seemed to be all alive, and the very clock on the chimney-piece (you know you can only see the back of it in the Looking-glass) had got the face of a little old man, and grinned at her.

'They don't keep this room so tidy as the other,' Alice thought to herself, as she noticed several of the chessmen down in the hearth among the cinders; but in another moment, with a little 'Oh!' of surprise, she was down on her hands and knees watching them. The chessmen were walking about, two and two!

'Here are the Red King and the Red Queen,' Alice said (in a

whisper, for fear of frightening them), 'and there are the White King and the White Queen sitting on the edge of the shovel – and here are two Castles walking arm in arm – I don't think they can hear me,' she went on, as she put her head closer down, 'and I'm nearly sure they ca'n't see me. I feel somehow as if I was getting invisible . . .'

Here something began squeaking on the table behind Alice, and made her turn her head just in time to see one of the White Pawns roll over and begin kicking: she watched it with great curiosity to see what would happen next.

'It is the voice of my child!' the White Queen cried out, as she rushed past the King, so violently that she knocked him over among the cinders. 'My precious Lily! My imperial kitten!' and she began scrambling wildly up the side of the fender.

'Imperial fiddlestick!' said the King, rubbing his nose, which had been hurt by the fall. He had a right to be a *little* annoyed with the Queen, for he was covered with ashes from head to foot.

Alice was very anxious to be of use, and, as the poor little Lily was nearly screaming herself into a fit, she hastily picked up the Queen and set her on the table by the side of her noisy little daughter.

The Queen gasped, and sat down: the rapid journey through the air had quite taken away her breath, and for a minute or two she could do nothing but hug the little Lily in silence. As soon as she had recovered her breath a little, she called out to the White King, who was sitting sulkily among the ashes, 'Mind the volcano!'

'What volcano?' said the King, looking up anxiously into the fire, as if he thought that was the most likely place to find one.

'Blew – me – up,' panted the Queen, who was still a little out of breath. 'Mind you come up – the regular way – don't get blown up!'

Alice watched the White King as he slowly struggled up from bar to bar, till at last she said 'Why, you'll be hours and hours getting to the table, at that rate. I'd far better help you, hadn't I?'

But the King took no notice of the question: it was quite clear that he could neither hear her nor see her.

So Alice picked him up very gently, and lifted him across more slowly than she had lifted the Queen, that she mightn't take his breath away; but, before she put him on the table, she thought she might as well dust him a little, he was so covered with ashes.

She said afterwards that she had never seen in all her life such a face as the King made, when he found himself held in the air by an invisible hand, and being dusted: he was far too much astonished to cry out, but his eyes and his mouth went on getting larger and larger, and rounder and rounder, till her hand shook so with laughing that she nearly let him drop upon the floor.

'Oh! *please* don't make such faces, my dear!' she cried out, quite forgetting that the King couldn't hear her. 'You make me laugh so that I can hardly hold you! And don't keep your mouth so wide open! All the ashes will get into it – there, now I think you're tidy enough!' she added, as she smoothed his hair, and set him upon the table near the Queen.

The King immediately fell flat on his back, and lay perfectly still; and Alice was a little alarmed at what she had done, and went round the room to see if she could find any water to throw over him. However, she could find nothing but a bottle of ink, and when she got back with it she found he had recovered, and he and the Queen were talking together in a frightened whisper – so low, that Alice could hardly hear what they said.

The King was saying 'I assure you, my dear, I turned cold to the very ends of my whiskers!'

To which the Queen replied 'You haven't got any whiskers.'

'The horror of that moment,' the King went on, 'I shall never, *never* forget!'

'You will, though,' the Queen said, 'if you don't make a memorandum of it.'

Alice looked on with great interest as the King took an enormous memorandum-book out of his pocket, and began writing. A sudden thought struck her, and she took hold of the end of the pencil, which came some way over his shoulder, and began writing for him.

The poor King looked puzzled and unhappy, and struggled with the pencil for some time without saying anything; but Alice was too strong for him, and at last he panted out 'My dear! I really *must* get a thinner pencil. I ca'n't manage this one a bit: it writes all manner of things that I don't intend . . .'

'What manner of things?' said the Queen, looking over the book (in which Alice had put "*The White Knight is sliding down the poker. He balances very badly*"). 'That's not a memorandum of *your* feelings!'

There was a book lying near Alice on the table, and while she sat watching the White King (for she was still a little anxious about him, and had the ink all ready to throw over him, in case he fainted again), she turned over the leaves, to find some part that she could read, '– for it's all in some language I don't know,' she said to herself.

It was like this.

JABBERWOCKY

'Twas brillig, and the slithy toves
Did gyre and gimble in the wabe:
All mimsy were the borogoves,
And the mome raths outgrabe.

She puzzled over this for some time, but at last a bright thought struck her. 'Why, it's a Looking-glass book, of course! And, if I hold it up to a glass, the words will all go the right way again.'

This was the poem that Alice read.

JABBERWOCKY

'Twas brillig, and the slithy toves
Did gyre and gimble in the wabe:
All mimsy were the borogoves,
And the mome raths outgrabe.

'Beware the Jabberwock, my son!
The jaws that bite, the claws that catch!
Beware the Jubjub bird, and shun
The frumious Bandersnatch!'

He took his vorpal sword in hand:
Long time the manxome foe he sought—
So rested he by the Tumtum tree,
And stood awhile in thought.

And, as in uffish thought he stood,
The Jabberwock, with eyes of flame,
Came whiffling through the tulgey wood,
And burbled as it came!

One, two! One, two! And through and through
The vorpal blade went snicker-snack!
He left it dead, and with its head
He went galumphing back.

'And, hast thou slain the Jabberwock?
Come to my arms, my beamish boy!
O frabjous day! Callooh! Callay!'
He chortled in his joy.

'Twas brillig, and the slithy toves
Did gyre and gimble in the wabe:
All mimsy were the borogoves,
And the mome raths outgrabe.

'It seems very pretty,' she said when she had finished it, 'but it's *rather* hard to understand!' (You see she didn't like to confess, even to herself, that she couldn't make it out at all.) 'Somehow it seems to fill my head with ideas – only I don't exactly know what they are! However, *somebody* killed *something*: that's clear, at any rate . . .'

'But oh!' thought Alice, suddenly jumping up, 'if I don't make haste, I shall have to go back through the Looking-glass, before I've seen what the rest of the house is like! Let's have a look at the garden first!' She was out of the room in a moment, and ran down stairs – or, at least, it wasn't exactly running, but a new invention for getting down stairs quickly and easily, as Alice said to herself. She just kept the tips of her fingers on the hand-rail, and floated gently down without even touching the stairs with her feet: then she floated on through the hall, and would have gone straight out at the door in the same way, if she hadn't caught hold of the door-post. She was getting a little giddy with so much floating in the air, and was rather glad to find herself walking again in the natural way.

SUN-TZU

from *The Art of War*

Forms and Dispositions

Master Sun said:

Of old,
    The Skilful Warrior
    First ensured
    His own
    Invulnerability;
    Then he waited for
    The enemy's
    Vulnerability.

Invulnerability rests
    With self;
    Vulnerability,
    With the enemy.

The Skilful Warrior
    Can achieve
    His own
    Invulnerability;
    But he can never bring about
    The enemy's
    Vulnerability.

Hence the saying
　'One can know
　Victory
　And yet not achieve it.'

Invulnerability is
　Defence;
　Vulnerability is
　Attack.

Defence implies
　Lack;
　Attack implies
　Abundance.

A Skilful Defender
　Hides beneath
　The Ninefold Earth;
　A Skilful Attacker
　Moves above
　The Ninefold Heaven.

Thus they achieve
　Protection
　And victory
　Intact.

To foresee
　The ordinary victory
　Of the common man
　Is no true skill.

To be victorious in battle
And to be acclaimed
For one's skill
Is no true
Skill.

To lift autumn fur
Is no
Strength;
To see sun and moon
Is no
Perception;
To hear thunder
Is no
Quickness of hearing.

The Skilful Warrior of old
Won
Easy victories.

The victories
Of the Skilful Warrior
Are not
Extraordinary victories;
They bring
Neither fame for wisdom
Nor merit for valour.

His victories
Are
Flawless;
His victory is
Flawless
Because it is

Inevitable;
He vanquishes
An already defeated enemy.

The Skilful Warrior
Takes his stand
On invulnerable ground;
He lets slip no chance
Of defeating the enemy.

The victorious army
Is victorious first
And seeks battle later;
The defeated army
Does battle first
And seeks victory later.

The Skilful Strategist
Cultivates
The Way
And preserves
The law;
Thus he is master
Of victory and defeat.

In War,
There are Five Steps:

Measurement,
Estimation,
Calculation,
Comparison,
Victory.

Earth determines
    Measurement;
    Measurement determines
    Estimation;
    Estimation determines
    Calculation;
    Calculation determines
    Comparison;
    Comparison determines
    Victory.

A victorious army
    Is like a pound weight
    In the scale against
    A grain;
A defeated army
    Is like a grain
    In the scale against
    A pound weight.

A victorious army
    Is like
    Pent-up water
    Crashing
    A thousand fathoms
    Into a gorge.

This is all
    A matter of
    Forms and
    Dispositions.

EARTH

Introduction

Earth. The earth, square and steady, strong and quite solid, gives a firm basis to our actions and bears all kinds of births. It is the place of the grotto, of the mountain, of the rocks and deserts, all places where something quite new can appear and grow. It is, too, the figure of the Great Mother, the eternal Virgin, and the womb of all humankind. But it can also be the place of decay, of stagnation and despair. Earth is linked to the cold, and to the melancholic temper. Dark and cold, but able to give birth to all life. The earth is like an underground temple, disquieting and essential, where every path converges and meets. It is like the winter of the world, when everything seems to be dead, but when in fact new life awaits. It is like the vibrant preparation of spring, hidden in the depths of caves. But, indeed, fertility itself inhabits the earth, like an eternal promise of renewal.

Oscar Wilde, in his *De Profundis*, expresses the extreme despair of being abandoned to himself and discovering the secret chambers of his soul. But one has to struggle with these thoughts in the most courageous way in order to overcome them. Bram Stoker's *Dracula* shows us the darkness of the human soul and the risk of the loss of humanity. When the 'master' Dracula approaches, the servant becomes mad and discovers new parts of himself, but without any kind of protection. We find the brilliant essay of Hannah Arendt on Eichmann going even deeper into degradation. The figure of the monster turns itself into something much more trivial, and, because of this, becomes even more monstrous. What can evil be? How can it really exist? This seems to be the question Arendt asks herself. Sometimes, the monster can just turn himself into a clown . . . but a deadly one. Fortunately, we go out of the prison and into open space with Yeats's poems: refreshing and hopeful, the pleasures and security of a renewed earth tell us the beauty of the future and the promises of a new land. This simplicity tells us, too, of the origin of time and the very inception of human history. A new departure is always possible, as we can experience it with *Lady Chatterley*. The waltz of the seasons and the song of desire melt together to form a powerful hymn to earthly delights, magnified by some scattered flowers over a womb. Rain, too, and the delicacy of kisses melt to create a unique scenery of love and affection. Thus the earth can redeem a life, regenerate bodies and give hope.

OSCAR WILDE

from *De Profundis*

Am I right in saying that hate blinds people? Do you see it now?
If you don't, try to see it.

How clearly I saw it then, as now, I need not tell you. But I
said to myself: 'At all costs, I must keep love in my heart. If I go
into prison without love what will become of my soul?' The
letters I wrote to you at that time from Holloway were my effort
to keep love as the dominant note of my own nature. I could if
I had chosen have torn you to pieces with bitter reproaches. I
could have rent you with maledictions. I could have held up a
mirror to you, and shown you such an image of yourself that
you would not have recognized it as your own till you found it
mimicking back your gestures of horror, and then you would
have known whose shape it was, and hated it and yourself for
ever. More than that indeed. The sins of another were being
placed to my account. Had I so chosen, I could on either trial
have saved myself at his expense, not from shame indeed, but
from imprisonment. Had I cared to show that the Crown witnesses
– the three most important – had been carefully coached by your
father and his solicitors, not in reticences merely, but in assertions,
in the absolute transference, deliberate, plotted and rehearsed,
of the actions and doings of someone else on to me, I could have
had each one of them dismissed from the box by the judge, more
summarily than even wretched perjured Atkins was. I could have
walked out of Court with my tongue in my cheek, and my hands
in my pockets, a free man. The strongest pressure was put upon

me to do so. I was earnestly advised, begged, entreated to do so by people whose sole interest was my welfare, and the welfare of my house. But I refused. I did not choose to do so. I have never regretted my decision for a single moment, even in the most bitter periods of my imprisonment. Such a course of action would have been beneath me. Sins of the flesh are nothing. They are maladies for physicians to cure, if they should be cured. Sins of the soul alone are shameful. To have secured my acquittal by such means would have been a lifelong torture to me. But do you really think that you were worthy of the love I was showing you then, or that for a single moment I thought you were? Do you really think that at any period in our friendship you were worthy of the love I showed you, or that for a single moment I thought you were? I knew you were not. But love does not traffic in a market place, nor use a huckster's scales. Its joy, like the joy of the intellect, is to feel alive. The aim of love is to love: no more, and no less. You were my enemy: such an enemy as no man ever had. I had given you my life: and to gratify the lowest and most contempt-ible of all human passions, Hatred and Vanity and Greed, you had thrown it away. In less than three years you had entirely ruined me from every point of view. For my own sake there was nothing for me to do but to love you. I knew that if I allowed myself to hate you that in the dry desert of existence over which I had to travel, and am travelling still, every rock would lose its shadow, every palm tree be withered, every well of water prove poisoned at its source. Are you beginning now to understand a little? Is your imagination awakening from the long lethargy in which it has lain? You know already what hate is. Is it beginning to dawn on you what love is and what is the nature of love? It is not too late for you to learn, though to teach it to you I may have had to go to a convict's cell.

After my terrible sentence, when the prison dress was on me, and the prison house closed, I sat amidst the ruins of my wonder-ful life, crushed by anguish, bewildered with terror, dazed through pain. But I would not hate you. Every day I said to myself: 'I must keep love in my heart to-day, else how shall I live through the day?' I reminded myself that you meant no evil, to me at any rate: I set myself to think that you had but drawn a bow at a venture, and that the arrow had pierced a king between the joints of his harness. To have weighed you against the smallest of my sorrows, the meanest of my losses, would have been, I felt, unfair. I determined I would regard you as one suffering too. I forced myself to believe that at last the scales had fallen from your long-blinded eyes. I used to fancy and with pain what your horror must have been when you contemplated your terrible handiwork. There were times, even in those dark days, the darkest of all my life, when I actually longed to console you, so sure was I that at last you had realized what you had done.

It did not occur to me then that you could have the supreme vice, shallowness. Indeed it was a real grief to me when I had to let you know that. I was obliged to reserve for my family business my first opportunity of receiving a letter: but my brother-in-law had written to me to say that if I would only write once to my wife she would, for my own sake and for our children's sake, take no action for divorce. I felt my duty was to do so. Setting aside other reasons, I could not bear the idea of being separated from Cyril, that beautiful, loving, lovable child of mine, my friend of all friends, my companion beyond all companions, one single hair of whose little golden head should have been dearer and more valuable to me than, I will not say you from top to toe, but the entire chrysolite of the whole world: was so indeed to me always, though I failed to understand it till too late.

Two weeks after your application, I get news of you. Robert Sherard, that bravest and most chivalrous of all brilliant beings, comes to see me, and among other things tells me that in that ridiculous *Mercure de France*, with its absurd affectation of being the true centre of literary corruption, you are about to publish an article on me with specimens of my letters. He asks me if it really was by my wish. I was greatly taken aback, and much annoyed, and gave orders that the thing was to be stopped at once. You had left my letters lying about for blackmailing companions to steal, for hotel servants to pilfer, for housemaids to sell. That was simply your careless want of appreciation of what I had written to you. But that you should seriously propose to publish selections from the balance was almost incredible to me. And which of my letters were they? I could get no information. That was my first news of you. It displeased me.

The second piece of news followed shortly afterwards. Your father's solicitors had appeared in prison, and served me with a bankruptcy notice for a paltry £700, the amount of their taxed costs. I was adjudged a public insolvent and ordered to be produced in Court. I felt most strongly, and feel still, and will revert to the subject again, that these costs should have been paid by your family. You had taken personally on yourself the responsibility of stating that your family would do so. It was that which had made the solicitor take up the case in the way he did. You were absolutely responsible. Even irrespective of your engagement on your family's behalf you should have felt that as you had brought the whole ruin on me, the least that could have been done was to spare me the additional ignominy of bankruptcy for an absolutely contemptible sum of money, less than half of what I spent on you in three brief summer months at Goring. Of that, however, no more here. I did, through the solicitor's clerk, I fully admit, receive a message from you on the subject, or at any rate in connection with the occasion. The day he came to receive my depositions and statements, he leant across the table – the prison warder being present – and, having consulted a piece of paper which he pulled from his pocket, said to me in a low voice: 'Prince Fleur de Lys wishes to be remembered to you.' I stared at him. He repeated the message again. I did not know what he meant. 'The gentleman is abroad at present,' he added mysteriously. It all flashed across me, and I remember that, for the first and last time in my entire prison life, I laughed. In that laugh was all the scorn of all the world. Prince Fleur de Lys! I saw – and subsequent events showed me that I rightly saw – that nothing that had happened had made you realize a single thing. You were in your own eyes still the graceful prince of a trivial comedy, not the sombre figure of a tragic show. All that had occurred was as but a feather for the cap that gilds a narrow head, a flower to pink the doublet that hides the heart that hate, and hate alone, can warm, that love, and love alone, finds cold. Prince Fleur de Lys! You were, no doubt, quite right to communicate with me under an assumed name. I myself, at that time, had no name at all. In the great prison where I was then incarcerated, I was merely the figure and letter of a little cell in a long gallery, one of a thousand lifeless numbers, as of a thousand lifeless lives. But surely there were many real names in real history which would have suited you much better, and by which I would have had no difficulty at all in recognizing you at once? I did not look for you behind the spangles of a tinsel vizard suitable only for an amusing masquerade. Ah! had your soul been, as for its own perfection even it should have been, wounded with sorrow, bowed with remorse, and humble with grief, such was not the disguise it would have chosen beneath whose shadow to seek entrance to the House of Pain! The great things of life are what they seem to be, and for that reason, strange as it may sound to you, are often difficult to interpret. But the little things of life are symbols. We receive our bitter lessons most easily through them. Your seemingly casual choice of a feigned name was, and will remain, symbolic. It reveals you.

Six weeks later a third piece of news arrives. I am called out of the hospital ward, where I was lying wretchedly ill, to receive a special message from you through the Governor of the Prison. He reads me out a letter you had addressed to him in which you stated that you proposed to publish an article 'on the case of Mr Oscar Wilde' in the *Mercure de France* (a 'magazine', you added for some extraordinary reason, 'corresponding to the English

Fortnightly Review') and were anxious to obtain my permission to publish extracts and selections from . . . what letters? The letters I had written you from Holloway Prison: the letters that should have been to you things sacred and secret beyond anything in the whole world! These actually were the letters you proposed to publish for the jaded *décadent* to wonder at, for the greedy *feuilletoniste* to chronicle, for the little lions of the *Quartier Latin* to gape and mouth at. Had there been nothing in your own heart to cry out against so vulgar a sacrilege you might at least have remembered the sonnet he wrote who saw with such sorrow and scorn the letters of John Keats sold by public auction in London and have understood at last the real meaning of my lines

> . . . I think they love not Art
> Who break the crystal of a poet's heart
> That small and sickly eyes may glare and gloat.

For what was your article to show? That I had been too fond of you? The Paris *gamin* was quite aware of the fact. They all read the newspapers, and most of them write for them. That I was a man of genius? The French understood that, and the peculiar quality of my genius, much better than you did, or could have been expected to do. That along with genius goes often a curious perversity of passion and desire? Admirable: but the subject belongs to Lombroso rather than to you. Besides, the patho-logical phenomenon in question is found also amongst those who have not genius. That in your war of hate with your father I was at once shield and weapon to each of you? Nay more, that in that hideous hunt for my life, that took place when the war was over, he never could have reached me had not your nets been already about my feet? Quite true: but I am told that Henri Bauer had already done it extremely well. Besides, to corroborate his view, had such been your intention, you did not require to publish my letters: at any rate those written from Holloway Prison.

Will you say, in answer to my questions, that in one of my Holloway letters I had myself asked you to try, as far as you were able, to set me a little right with some small portion of the world? Certainly, I did so. Remember how and why I am here at this very moment. Do you think I am here on account of my relations with the witnesses on my trial? My relations, real or supposed, with people of that kind were matters of no interest either to the Government or to Society. They knew nothing of them and cared less. I am here for having tried to put your father into prison. My attempt failed, of course. My own Counsel threw up their briefs. Your father completely turned the tables on me, and had me in prison, has me there still. That is why there is contempt felt for me. That is why people despise me. That is why I have to serve out every day, every hour, every minute of my dreadful imprisonment. That is why my petitions have been refused.

You were the only person who, and without in any way exposing yourself to scorn or danger or blame, could have given another colour to the whole affair, have put the matter in a different light, have shown to a certain degree how things really stood. I would not, of course, have expected, nor indeed wished you to have stated how and for what purpose you had sought my assistance in your trouble at Oxford: or how, and for what purpose, if you had a purpose at all, you had practically never left my side for nearly three years. My incessant attempts to break off a friendship that was so ruinous to me as an artist, as a man of position, as a member of Society even, need not have been chronicled with the accuracy with which they have been set down here. Nor would I have desired you to have described the scenes you used to make with such almost monotonous recurrence: nor to have reprinted your wonderful series of telegrams to me with their strange mixture of romance and finance: nor to have quoted from letters the more revolting or heartless passages as I have been forced to do. Still, I thought it would have been good, as well for you as for me, if you had made some protest against your father's version of our friendship, one no less grotesque than venomous and as absurd in its inference to you as it was dishonouring in its reference to me. That version has now actually passed into serious history: it is quoted, believed, and chronicled: the preacher has taken it for his text, and the moralist for his barren theme: and I who appealed to all the ages have had to accept my verdict from one who is an ape and a buffoon. I have said, and with some bitterness, I admit, in this letter that such was the irony of things that your father would live to be the hero of a Sunday school tract: that you would rank with the infant Samuel: and that my place would be between Gilles de Retz and the Marquis de Sade. I dare say it is best so. I have no desire to complain. One of the many lessons that one learns in prison is, that things are what they are and will be what they will be. Nor have I any doubt that the leper of medievalism and the author of *Justine* will prove better company than *Sandford and Merton*.

But at the time I wrote to you I felt that for both our sakes it would be a good thing, a proper thing, a right thing, not to accept that account which your father had put forward through his Counsel for the edification of a Philistine world, and that is why I asked you to think out and write something that would be nearer the truth. It would at least have been better for you than scribbling to the French papers about the domestic life of your parents. What did the French care whether or not your parents had led a happy domestic life? One cannot conceive a subject more entirely un-interesting to them. What did interest them was how an artist of my distinction, one who by the school and movement of which he was the incarnation had exercised a marked influence on the direction of French thought, could, having led such a life, have brought such an action. Had you proposed for your article to publish the letters, endless I fear in number, in which I had spoken to you of the ruin you were bringing on my life, of the madness of moods of rage that you were allowing to master you to your own hurt as well as to mine, and of my desire, nay, my determination to end a friendship so fatal to me in every way, I could have understood it, though I would not have allowed such letters to be published: when your father's Counsel desiring to catch me in a contradiction suddenly produced in Court a letter of mine, written to you in March 1893, in which I stated that, rather than endure a repetition of the hideous scenes you seemed to take such a terrible pleasure in making, I would readily consent to be 'blackmailed by every renter in London', it was a very real grief to me that that side of my friendship with you should inadvertently be revealed to the common gaze: but that you should have been so slow to see, so lacking in all sensitiveness, and so dull in apprehension of what is rare, delicate and beautiful, as to propose yourself to publish the letters in which and through which I was trying to keep alive the very spirit and soul of love, that it might dwell in my body through the long years of that body's humiliation – this was, and still is to me a source of the very deepest pain, the most poignant disappointment. Why you did so, I fear I know but too well. If hate blinded your eyes, vanity sewed your eyelids together with threads of iron. The 'faculty by which, and by which alone, one can understand others in their real as in their ideal relations' your narrow egotism had blunted, and long disuse had made of no avail. The imagination was as much in prison as I was. Vanity had barred up the windows, and the name of the warder was hate.

All this took place in the early part of November of the year before last. A great river of life flows between me and a date so distant. Hardly, if at all, can you see across so wide a waste. But to me it seems to have occurred, I will not say yesterday, but to-day. Suffering is one very long moment. We cannot divide it by seasons. We can only record its moods, and chronicle their return. With us time itself does not progress. It revolves. It seems to circle round one centre of pain. The paralysing immobility of a life every circumstance of which is regulated after an unchangeable pattern, so that we eat and drink and lie down and pray, or kneel at least for prayer, according to the inflexible laws of an iron formula: this immobile quality, that makes each dreadful day in the very minutest detail like its brother, seems to communicate itself to those external forces, the very essence of whose existence is ceaseless change. Of seed-time or harvest, of the reapers bending over the corn, or the grape gatherers threading through the vines, of the grass in the orchard made white with broken blossoms or strewn with fallen fruit: of these we know nothing, and can know nothing.

For us there is only one season, the season of sorrow. The very sun and moon seem taken from us. Outside, the day may be blue and gold, but the light that creeps down through the thickly muffled glass of the small iron-barred window beneath which one sits is grey and niggard. It is always twilight in one's cell, as it is always twilight in one's heart. And in the sphere of thought, no less than in the sphere of time, motion is no more. The thing that you personally have long ago forgotten, or can easily forget, is happening to me now, and will happen to me again to-morrow. Remember this, and you will be able to understand a little of why I am writing, and in this manner writing . . .

A week later, I am transferred here. Three more months go over and my mother dies. No one knew better than you how deeply I loved and honoured her. Her death was terrible to me; but I, once a lord of language, have no words in which to express my anguish and my shame. Never even in the most perfect days of my development as an artist could I have found words fit to bear so august a burden; or to move with sufficient stateliness of music through the purple pageant of my incommunicable woe. She and my father had bequeathed me a name they had made noble and honoured, not merely in literature, art, archaeology, and science, but in the public history of my own country, in its evolution as a nation. I had disgraced that name eternally. I had made it a low byword among low people. I had dragged it through the very mire. I had given it to brutes that they might make it brutal, and to fools that they might turn it into a synonym for folly. What I suffered then, and still suffer, is not for pen to write or paper to record. My wife, always kind and gentle to me, rather than that I should hear the news from indifferent lips, travelled, ill as she was, all the way from Genoa to England to break to me herself the tidings of so irreparable, so irredeemable, a loss. Messages of sympathy reached me from all who had still affection for me. Even people who had not known me personally, hearing that a new sorrow had broken into my life, wrote to ask that some expression of their condolence should be conveyed to me . . .

Three months go over. The calendar of my daily conduct and labour that hangs on the outside of my cell door, with my name and sentence written upon it, tells me that it is May.

My friends come to see me again. I enquire, as I always do, after you. I am told that you are in your villa at Naples, and are bringing out a volume of poems. At the close of the interview it is mentioned casually that you are dedicating them to me. The tidings seemed to give me a sort of nausea of life. I said nothing, but silently went back to my cell with contempt and scorn in my heart. How could you dream of dedicating a volume of poems to me without first asking my permission? Dream, do I say? How could you dare do such a thing? Will you give as your answer that in the days of my greatness and fame I had consented to receive the dedication of your early work? Certainly I did so: just as I would have accepted the homage of any other young men beginning the difficult and beautiful art of literature. All homage is delightful to an artist and doubly sweet when youth brings it. Laurel and bay leaf wither when aged hands pluck them. Only youth has a right to crown an artist. That is the real privilege of being young if youth only knew it. But the days of abasement and infamy are different from those of greatness and fame. You had yet to learn that.

Prosperity, pleasure and success, may be rough of grain and common in fibre, but sorrow is the most sensitive of all created things. There is nothing that stirs in the whole world of thought to which sorrow does not vibrate in terrible and exquisite pulsation. The thin beaten-out leaf of tremulous gold that chronicles the direction of forces the eye cannot see is in comparison coarse. It is a wound that bleeds when any hand but that of love touches it, and even then must bleed again, though not in pain.

You could write to the Governor of Wandsworth Prison to ask my permission to publish my letters in the *Mercure de France*, 'corresponding to our English *Fortnightly Review*'. Why not have written to the Governor of the Prison at Reading to ask my permission to dedicate your poems to me, whatever fantastic description you may have chosen to give them? Was it because in the one case the magazine in question had been prohibited by me from publishing letters, the legal copyright of which, as you are, of course, perfectly well aware, was and is vested entirely in me, and in the other you thought that you could enjoy the wilfulness of your own way without my knowing anything about it till it was too late to interfere? The mere fact that I was a man disgraced, ruined and in prison should have made you, if you desired to write my name on the fore-page of your work, beg it of me as a favour, an honour, a privilege: that is the way in which one should approach those who are in distress and sit in shame.

Where there is sorrow there is holy ground. Some day people will realize what that means. They will know nothing of life till they do. Robbie and natures like his can realize it. When I was brought down from my prison to the Court of Bankruptcy, between two policemen, Robbie waited in the long dreary corridor that, before the whole crowd, whom an action so sweet and simple hushed into silence, he might gravely raise his hat to me, as, handcuffed and with bowed head, I passed him by. Men have gone to heaven for smaller things than that. It was in this spirit, and with this mode of love, that the saints knelt down to wash the feet of the poor, or stooped to kiss the leper on the cheek. I have never said one single word to him about what he did. I do

74

not know to the present moment whether he is aware that I was even conscious of his action. It is not a thing for which one can render formal thanks in formal words. I store it in the treasure-house of my heart. I keep it there as a secret debt that I am glad to think I can never possibly repay. It is embalmed and kept sweet by the myrrh and cassia of many tears. When wisdom has been profitless to me, philosophy barren, and the proverbs and phrases of those who have sought to give me consolation as dust and ashes in my mouth, the memory of that little, lovely, silent act of love has unsealed for me all the wells of pity: made the desert blossom like a rose, and brought me out of the bitterness of lonely exile into harmony with the wounded, broken, and great heart of the world. When people are able to understand, not merely how beautiful Robbie's action was, but why it meant so much to me, and always will mean so much, then, perhaps, they will realize how and in what spirit they should approach me . . .

BRAM STOKER

from *Dracula*

Dr Seward's Diary

5 June – The case of Renfield grows more interesting the more I get to understand the man. He has certain qualities very largely developed: selfishness, secrecy and purpose. I wish I could get at what is the object of the latter. He seems to have some settled scheme of his own, but what it is I do not yet know. His redeeming quality is a love of animals, though, indeed, he has such curious turns in it that I sometimes imagine he is only abnormally cruel. His pets are of odd sorts. Just now his hobby is catching flies. He has at present such a quantity that I have had myself to expostulate. To my astonishment, he did not break out into a fury, as I expected, but took the matter in simple seriousness. He thought for a moment, and then said: 'May I have three days? I shall clear them away.' Of course, I said that would do. I must watch him.

18 June – He has turned his mind now to spiders, and has got several very big fellows in a box. He keeps feeding them with his flies, and the number of the latter is becoming sensibly diminished, although he has used half his food in attracting more flies from outside to his room.

1 July – His spiders are now becoming as great a nuisance as his flies, and today I told him that he must get rid of them. He looked very sad at this, so I said that he must clear out some of them, at all events. He cheerfully acquiesced in this, and I gave him the same time as before for reduction. He disgusted me much while with him, for when a horrid blow-fly, bloated with some carrion food, buzzed into the room, he caught it, held it exultingly for a few moments between his finger and thumb, and, before I knew what he was going to do, put it in his mouth and ate it. I scolded him for it, but he argued quietly that it was very good and very wholesome; that it was life, strong life, and gave life to him. This gave me an idea; or the rudiment of one. I must watch how he gets rid of his spiders. He has evidently some deep problem in his mind, for he keeps a little notebook in which he is always jotting down something. Whole pages of it are filled with masses of figures, generally single numbers added up in batches, and then the totals added in batches again, as though he were 'focusing' some account, as the auditors put it.

8 July – There is a method in his madness, and the rudimentary idea in my mind is growing. It will be a whole idea soon, and then, oh, unconscious cerebration! you will have to give the wall to your conscious brother. I kept away from my friend for a few days, so that I might notice if there were any change. Things remain as they were except that he has parted with some of his pets and got a new one. He has managed to get a sparrow, and has already partially tamed it. His means of taming is simple, for already the spiders have diminished. Those that do remain, however, are well fed, for he still brings in the flies by tempting them with his food.

19 July – We are progressing. My friend has now a whole colony of sparrows, and his flies and spiders are almost obliterated. When I came in he ran to me and said he wanted to ask me a great favour – a very, very great favour; and as he spoke he fawned on me like a dog. I asked him what it was, and he said, with a sort of rapture in his voice and bearing:

'A kitten, a nice little, sleek, playful kitten, that I can play with, and teach, and feed – and feed – and feed!' I was not unprepared for this request, for I had noticed how his pets went on increasing in size and vivacity, but I did not care that his pretty family of tame sparrows should be wiped out in the same manner as the flies and the spiders; so I said I would see about it, and asked him if he would not rather have a cat than a kitten. His eagerness betrayed him as he answered:

'Oh yes, I would like a cat! I only asked for a kitten lest you should refuse me a cat. No one would refuse me a kitten, would they?' I shook my head, and said that at present I feared it would not be possible, but that I would see about it. His face fell, and I could see a warning of danger in it, for there was a sudden fierce, sidelong look which meant killing. The man is an undeveloped homicidal maniac. I shall test him with his present craving and see how it will work out; then I shall know more.

10 p.m. – I have visited him again and found him sitting in a corner brooding. When I came in he threw himself on his knees before me and implored me to let him have a cat; that his salvation depended upon it. I was firm, however, and told him that he could not have it, whereupon he went without a word, and sat down, gnawing his fingers, in the corner where I had found him. I shall see him in the morning early.

20 July – Visited Renfield very early, before the attendant went his rounds. Found him up and humming a tune. He was spreading out his sugar, which he had saved, in the window, and was manifestly beginning his fly-catching again; and beginning it cheerfully and with a good grace. I looked around for his birds, and not seeing them, asked him where they were. He replied, without turning round, that they had all flown away. There were a few feathers about the room and on his pillow a drop of blood. I said nothing, but went and told the keeper to report to me if there were anything odd about him during the day.

11 a.m. – The attendant has just been to me to say that Renfield has been very sick and has disgorged a whole lot of feathers. 'My belief is, doctor,' he said, 'that he has eaten his birds, and that he just took and ate them raw!'

11 p.m. – I gave Renfield a strong opiate tonight, enough to make even him sleep, and took away his pocket-book to look at it. The thought that has been buzzing about my brain lately is complete, and the theory proved. My homicidal maniac is of a peculiar kind. I shall have to invent a new classification for him, and call him a zoophagous (life-eating) maniac; what he desires is to absorb as many lives as he can, and he has laid himself out to achieve it in a cumulative way. He gave many flies to one spider and many spiders to one bird, and then wanted a cat to eat the many birds. What would have been his later steps? It would almost be worth while to complete the experiment. It might be done if there were only a sufficient cause. Men sneered at vivisection, and yet look at its results today! Why not advance science in its most difficult and vital aspect – the knowledge of the brain? Had I even the secret of one such mind – did I hold the key to the fancy of even one lunatic – I might advance my own branch of science to a pitch compared with which Burdon-Sanderson's physiology or Ferrier's brain-knowledge would be as nothing. If only there were a sufficient cause! I must not think too much of this, or I may be tempted; a good cause might turn the scale with me, for may not I too be of an exceptional brain, congenitally?

How well the man reasoned; lunatics always do within their own scope. I wonder at how many lives he values a man, or if at only one. He has closed the account most accurately, and today begun a new record. How many of us begin a new record with each day of our lives?

To me it seems only yesterday that my whole life ended with my new hope, and that truly I began a new record. So it will be until the Great Recorder sums me up and closes my ledger account with a balance to profit or loss. Oh, Lucy, Lucy, I cannot be angry with you, nor can I be angry with my friend whose happiness is yours; but I must only wait on hopeless and work. Work! work!

If I only could have as strong a cause as my poor mad friend there, a good, unselfish cause to make me work, that would be indeed happiness.

HANNAH ARENDT

from *Eichmann and the Holocaust*

What eventually led to his capture was his compulsion to talk big – he was 'fed up with being an anonymous wanderer between the worlds' – and this compulsion must have grown considerably stronger as time passed, not only because he had nothing to do that he could consider worth doing, but also because the postwar era had bestowed so much unexpected 'fame' upon him.

But bragging is a common vice, and a more specific, and also more decisive, flaw in Eichmann's character was his almost total inability ever to look at anything from the other fellow's point of view. Nowhere was this flaw more conspicuous than in his account of the Vienna episode. He and his men and the Jews were all 'pulling together', and whenever there were any difficulties the Jewish functionaries would come running to him 'to unburden their hearts', to tell him 'all their grief and sorrow', and to ask for his help. The Jews 'desired' to emigrate, and he, Eichmann, was there to help them, because it so happened that at the same time the Nazi authorities had expressed a desire to see their Reich *judenrein*. The two desires coincided, and he, Eichmann, could 'do justice to both parties'. At the trial, he never gave an inch when it came to this part of the story, although he agreed that today, when 'times have changed so much', the Jews might not be too happy to recall this 'pulling together' and he did not want 'to hurt their feelings'.

The German text of the taped police examination, conducted from 29 May 1960 to 17 January 1961, each page corrected and approved by Eichmann, constitutes a veritable gold mine for a psychologist – provided he is wise enough to understand that the horrible can be not only ludicrous but outright funny. Some of the comedy cannot be conveyed in English, because it lies in Eichmann's heroic fight with the German language, which invariably defeats him. It is funny when he speaks, *passim*, of 'winged words' (*geflügelte Worte*, a German colloquialism for famous quotes from the classics) when he means stock phrases, *Redensarten*, or slogans, *Schlagworte*. It was funny when, during the cross-examination on the Sassen documents, conducted in German by the presiding judge, he used the phrase '*kontra geben*' (to give tit for tat), to indicate that he had resisted Sassen's efforts to liven up his stories; Judge Landau, obviously ignorant of the mysteries of card games, did not understand, and Eichmann could not think of any other way to put it. Dimly aware of a defect that must have plagued him even in school – it amounted to a mild case of aphasia – he apologized, saying, 'Officialese [*Amtssprache*] is my only language.' But the point here is that officialese became his language because he was genuinely incapable of uttering a single sentence that was not a cliché. (Was it these clichés that the psychiatrists thought so 'normal' and 'desirable'? Are these the 'positive ideas' a clergyman hopes for in those to whose souls he ministers? Eichmann's best opportunity to show this positive side of his character in Jerusalem came when the young police officer in charge of his mental and psychological well-being handed him *Lolita* for relaxation. After two days Eichmann returned it, visibly indignant; 'Quite an unwholesome book' – '*Das ist aber ein sehr unerfreuliches Buch*' – he told his guard.) To be sure, the judges were right when they finally told the accused that all he had said was 'empty talk' – except that they thought the emptiness was feigned, and that the accused wished to cover up other thoughts which, though hideous, were not empty. This supposition seems refuted by the striking consistency with which Eichmann, despite his rather bad memory, repeated word for word the same stock phrases and self-invented clichés (when he did succeed in constructing a sentence of his own, he repeated it until it became a cliché) each time he referred to an incident or event of importance to him. Whether writing his memoirs in Argentina or in Jerusalem, whether speaking to the police examiner or to the court, what he said was always the same, expressed in the same words. The longer one listened to him, the more obvious it became that his inability to speak was closely connected with an inability to *think*, namely, to think from the standpoint of somebody else. No communication was possible with him, not because he lied but because he was surrounded by the most reliable of all safeguards against the words and the presence of others, and hence against reality as such.

Thus, confronted for eight months with the reality of being examined by a Jewish policeman, Eichmann did not have the slightest hesitation in explaining to him at considerable length, and repeatedly, why he had been unable to attain a higher grade in the SS, and that this was not his fault. He had done everything, even asked to be sent to active military duty – 'Off to the front, I said to myself, then the *Standartenführer* [colonelcy] will come quicker.' In court, on the contrary, he pretended he had asked to be transferred because he wanted to escape his murderous duties. He did not insist much on this, though, and, strangely, he was not confronted with his utterances to Captain Less, whom he also told that he had hoped to be nominated for the *Einsatzgruppen*, the mobile killing units in the East, because when they were formed, in March 1941, his office was 'dead' – there was no emigration any longer and deportations had not yet been started. There was, finally, his greatest ambition – to be promoted to the job of police chief in some German town; again, nothing doing. What makes these pages of the examination so funny is that all this was told in the tone of someone who was sure of finding 'normal, human' sympathy for a hard-luck story. 'Whatever I prepared and planned, everything went wrong, my personal affairs as well as my years-long efforts to obtain land and soil for the Jews. I don't know, everything was as if under an evil spell; whatever I desired and wanted and planned to do, fate prevented it somehow. I was frustrated in everything, no matter what.' When Captain Less asked his opinion on some damning and possibly lying evidence given by a former colonel of the SS, he exclaimed, suddenly stuttering with rage: 'I am very much surprised that this man could ever have been an SS *Standarten-führer*, that surprises me very much indeed. It is altogether, altogether unthinkable. I don't know what to say.' He never said these things in a spirit of defiance, as though he wanted, even now, to defend the standards by which he had lived in the past. The very words 'SS', or 'career', or 'Himmler' (whom he always called by his long official title: Reichsführer SS and Chief of the German Police, although he by no means admired him) triggered in him a mechanism that had become completely unalterable. The presence of Captain Less, a Jew from Germany and unlikely in any case to think that members of the SS advanced in their careers through the exercise of high moral qualities, did not for a moment throw this mechanism out of gear.

Now and then, the comedy breaks into the horror itself, and results in stories, presumably true enough, whose macabre humour easily surpasses that of any Surrealist invention. Such was the story told by Eichmann during the police examination about the unlucky Kommerzialrat Storfer of Vienna, one of the representatives of the Jewish community. Eichmann had received a telegram from Rudolf Höss, Commandant of Auschwitz, telling him that Storfer had arrived and had urgently requested to see Eichmann. 'I said to myself: OK, this man has always behaved well, that is worth my while . . . I'll go there myself and see what is the matter with him. And I go to Ebner [chief of the Gestapo in Vienna], and Ebner says – I remember it only vaguely – "If only he had not been so clumsy; he went into hiding and tried to escape," something of the sort. And the police arrested him and sent him to the concentration camp, and, according to the orders of the Reichsführer [Himmler], no one could get out once he was in. Nothing could be done, neither Dr Ebner nor I nor anybody else could do anything about it. I went to Auschwitz and asked Höss to see Storfer. "Yes, yes [Höss said], he is in one of the labour gangs." With Storfer afterward, well, it was normal and human, we had a normal, human encounter. He told me all his grief and sorrow. I said: 'Well, my dear old friend [*Ja, mein lieber guter Storfer*], we certainly got it! What rotten luck!' And I also said: 'Look, I really cannot help you, because according to orders from the Reichsführer nobody can get out. I can't get you out. Dr Ebner can't get you out. I hear you made a mistake, that you went into hiding or wanted to bolt, which, after all, *you* did not need to do.' [Eichmann meant that Storfer, as a Jewish functionary, had immunity from deportation.] I forget what his reply to this was. And then I asked him how he was. And he said, yes, he wondered if he couldn't be let off work, it was heavy work. And then I said to Höss: "Work – Storfer won't have to work!" But Höss said: "Everyone works here." So I said: "OK," I said, "I'll make out a chit to the effect that Storfer has to keep the gravel paths in order with a broom" – there were little gravel paths there – "and that he has the right to sit down with his broom on one of the benches." [To Storfer] I said: "Will that be all right, Mr Storfer? Will that suit you?" Whereupon he was very pleased, and we shook hands, and then he was given the broom and sat down on his bench. It was a great inner joy to me that I could at least see the man with whom I had worked for so many long years, and that we could speak with each other.' Six weeks after this normal human encounter, Storfer was dead – not gassed, apparently, but shot.

Is this a textbook case of bad faith, of lying self-deception combined with outrageous stupidity? Or is it simply the case of the eternally unrepentant criminal (Dostoevsky once mentions in his diaries that in Siberia, among scores of murderers, rapists and burglars, he never met a single man who would admit that he had done wrong) who cannot afford to face reality because his crime has become part and parcel of it? Yet Eichmann's case is different from that of the ordinary criminal, who can shield himself effectively against the reality of a non-criminal world only within the narrow limits of his gang. Eichmann needed only to recall the past in order to feel assured that he was not lying and that he was not deceiving himself, for he and the world he lived in had once been in perfect harmony. And that German society of eighty million people had been shielded against reality and factuality by exactly the same means, the same self-deception, lies and stupidity that had now become ingrained in Eichmann's mentality. These lies changed from year to year, and they frequently contradicted each other; moreover, they were not necessarily the same for the various branches of the Party hierarchy or the people at large. But the practice of self-deception had become so common, almost a moral prerequisite for survival, that even now, eighteen years after the collapse of the Nazi regime, when most of the specific content of its lies has been forgotten, it is sometimes difficult not to believe that mendacity has become an integral part of the German national character. During the war, the lie most effective with the whole of the German people was the slogan of 'the battle of destiny for the German people' (*der Schicksalskampf des deutschen Volkes*), coined either by Hitler or by Goebbels, which made self-deception easier on three counts: it suggested, first, that the war was no war; second, that it was started by destiny and not by Germany; and, third, that it was a matter of life and death for the Germans, who must annihilate their enemies or be annihilated.

Eichmann's astounding willingness, in Argentina as well as in Jerusalem, to admit his crimes was due less to his own criminal capacity for self-deception than to the aura of systematic mendacity that had constituted the general, and generally accepted, atmosphere of the Third Reich. 'Of course' he had played a role in the extermination of the Jews; of course if he 'had not transported them, they would not have been delivered to the butcher'. 'What,' he asked, 'is there to "admit"?' Now, he proceeded, he 'would like to find peace with [his] former enemies' – a sentiment he shared not only with Himmler, who had expressed it during the last year of the war, or with the Labour Front leader Robert Ley (who, before he committed suicide in Nuremberg, had proposed the establishment of a 'conciliation committee' consisting of the Nazis responsible for the massacres and the Jewish survivors) but also, unbelievably, with many ordinary Germans, who were heard to express themselves in exactly the same terms at the end of the war. This outrageous cliché was no longer issued to them from above, it was a self-fabricated stock phrase, as devoid of reality as those clichés by which the people had lived for twelve years; and you could almost see what an 'extraordinary sense of elation' it gave to the speaker the moment it popped out of his mouth.

Eichmann's mind was filled to the brim with such sentences. His memory proved to be quite unreliable about what had actually happened; in a rare moment of exasperation, Judge Landau asked the accused: 'What *can* you remember?' (if you don't remember the discussions at the so-called Wannsee Conference, which dealt with the various methods of killing) and the answer, of course, was that Eichmann remembered the turning points in his own career rather well, but that they did not necessarily coincide with the turning points in the story of Jewish extermination or, as a matter of fact, with the turning points in history. (He always had trouble remembering the exact date of the outbreak of the war or of the invasion of Russia.) But the point of the matter is that he had not forgotten a single one of the sentences of his that at one time or another had served to give him a 'sense of elation'. Hence, whenever, during the cross-examination, the judges tried to appeal to his conscience, they were met with 'elation', and they were outraged as well as disconcerted when they learned that the accused had at his disposal a different elating cliché for each period of his life and each of his activities. In his mind, there was no contradiction between 'I will jump into my grave laughing', appropriate for the end of the war, and 'I shall gladly hang myself in public as a warning example for all anti-Semites on this earth', which now, under vastly different circumstances, fulfilled exactly the same function of giving him a lift.

These habits of Eichmann's created considerable difficulty during the trial – less for Eichmann himself than for those who had come to prosecute him, to defend him, to judge him and to report on him. For all this, it was essential that one take him seriously, and this was very hard to do, unless one sought the easiest way out of the dilemma between the unspeakable horror of the deeds and the undeniable ludicrousness of the man who perpetrated them, and declared him a clever, calculating liar – which he obviously was not. His own convictions in this matter were far from modest: 'One of the few gifts fate bestowed upon me is a capacity for truth insofar as it depends upon myself.' This gift he had claimed even before the prosecutor wanted to settle on him crimes he had not committed. In the disorganized, rambling notes he made in Argentina in preparation for the interview with Sassen, when he was still, as he even pointed out at the time, 'in full possession of my physical and psychological freedom', he had issued a fantastic warning to 'future historians to be objective enough not to stray from the path of this truth recorded here' – fantastic because every line of these scribblings shows his utter ignorance of everything that was not directly, technically and bureaucratically connected with his job, and also shows an extraordinarily faulty memory.

Despite all the efforts of the prosecution, everybody could see that this man was not a 'monster', but it was difficult indeed not to suspect that he was a clown. And since this suspicion would have been fatal to the whole enterprise, and was also rather hard to sustain in view of the sufferings he and his like had caused to millions of people, his worst clowneries were hardly noticed and almost never reported. What could you do with a man who first declared, with great emphasis, that the one thing he had learned in an ill-spent life was that one should never take an oath ('Today no man, no judge could ever persuade me to make a sworn statement, to declare something under oath as a witness. I refuse it, I refuse it for moral reasons. Since my experience tells me that if one is loyal to his oath, one day he has to take the consequences, I have made up my mind once and for all that no judge in the world or any other authority will ever be capable of making me swear an oath, to give sworn testimony. I won't do it voluntarily and no one will be able to force me'), and then, after being told explicitly that if he wished to testify in his own defence he might 'do so under oath or without an oath', declared without further ado that he would prefer to testify under oath? Or who, repeatedly and with a great show of feeling, assured the court, as he had assured the police examiner, that the worst thing he could do would be to try to escape his true responsibilities, to fight for his neck, to plead for mercy – and then, upon instruction of his counsel, submitted a handwritten document, containing his plea for mercy?

As far as Eichmann was concerned, these were questions of changing moods, and as long as he was capable of finding, either in his memory or on the spur of the moment, an elating stock phrase to go with them, he was quite content, without ever becoming aware of anything like 'inconsistencies'. As we shall see, this horrible gift for consoling himself with clichés did not leave him in the hour of his death.

W.B. YEATS

from *Selected Poems*

He wishes for the Cloths of Heaven

Had I the heavens' embroidered cloths,
Enwrought with golden and silver light,
The blue and the dim and the dark cloths
Of night and light and the half-light,
I would spread the cloths under your feet:
But I, being poor, have only my dreams;
I have spread my dreams under your feet;
Tread softly because you tread on my dreams.

The Song of Wandering Aengus

I went out to the hazel wood,
Because a fire was in my head,
And cut and peeled a hazel wand,
And hooked a berry to a thread;
And when white moths were on the wing,
And moth-like stars were flickering out,
I dropped the berry in a stream
And caught a little silver trout.

When I had laid it on the floor
I went to blow the fire aflame,

But something rustled on the floor,
And some one called me by my name:
It had become a glimmering girl
With apple blossom in her hair
Who called me by my name and ran
And faded through the brightening air.

Though I am old with wandering
Through hollow lands and hilly lands,
I will find out where she has gone,
And kiss her lips and take her hands;
And walk among long dappled grass,
And pluck till time and times are done
The silver apples of the moon,
The golden apples of the sun.

D. H. LAWRENCE

from *Lady Chatterley's Lover*

'But I wouldn't preach to the men: only strip 'em an' say: Look at yourselves! That's workin' for money! – Hark at yourselves! That's working for money. You've been workin' for money! – Look at Tevershall! It's horrible. That's because it was built while you was working for money. – Look at your girls! They don't care about you, you don't care about them. It's because you've spent your time working and caring for money. You can't talk nor move nor live, you can't properly be with a woman. You're not alive. Look at yourselves!—'

There fell a complete silence. Connie was half listening, and threading in the hair at the root of his belly a few forget-me-nots that she had gathered on the way to the hut. Outside, the world had gone still, and a little icy.

'You've got four kinds of hair,' she said to him. 'On your chest it's nearly black, and your hair isn't dark on your head: but your moustache is hard and dark red, and your hair here, your love-hair, is like a little bush of bright red-gold mistletoe. It's the loveliest of all!'

He looked down and saw the milky bits of forget-me-nots in the hair on his groin.

'Ay! That's where to put forget-me-nots – in the man-hair, or the maiden-hair. – But don't you care about the future?'

She looked up at him.

'Oh, I do, terribly!' she said.

'Because when I feel the human world is doomed, has doomed

itself by its own mingy beastliness – then I feel the colonies aren't far enough. The moon wouldn't be far enough, because even there you could look back and see the earth, dirty, beastly, unsavoury among all the stars: made foul by men. Then I feel I've swallowed gall, and it's eating my inside out, and nowhere's far enough away to get away. – But when I get a turn, I forget it all again. Though it's a shame, what's been done to people these last hundred years: men turned into nothing but labour-insects, and all their manhood taken away, and all their real life. I'd wipe the machines off the face of the earth again, and end the industrial epoch absolutely, like a black mistake. But since I can't, an' nobody can, I'd better hold my peace, an' try an' live my own life: if I've got one to live, which I rather doubt.'

The thunder had ceased outside, and the rain, which had abated, suddenly came striking down, with a last blench of lightning and mutter of departing storm. Connie was uneasy. He had talked so long now – and he was really talking to himself, not to her. Despair seemed to come down on him completely, and she was feeling happy, she hated despair. She knew her leaving him, which he had only just realized inside himself, had plunged him back into this mood. And she triumphed a little.

She opened the door and looked at the straight heavy rain, like a steel curtain, and had a sudden desire to rush out into it, to rush away. She got up, and began swiftly pulling off her stockings, then her dress and underclothing, and he held his breath. Her pointed, keen animal breasts tipped and stirred as she moved. She was ivory-coloured in the greenish light. She slipped on her rubber shoes again and ran out with a wild little laugh, holding up her breasts to the heavy rain and spreading her arms, and running blurred in the rain with the eurythmic dance-movements she had learned so long ago in Dresden. It was a strange pallid figure lifting and falling, bending so the rain beat and glistened on the full haunches, swaying up again and coming belly-forward through the rain, then stooping again so that only the full loins and buttocks were offered in a kind of homage towards him, repeating a wild obeisance.

He laughed wryly, and threw off his clothes. It was too much. He jumped out, naked and white, with a little shiver, into the hard, slanting rain. Flossie sprang before him with a frantic little bark. Connie, her hair all wet and sticking to her head, turned her hot face and saw him. Her blue eyes blazed with excitement, as she turned and ran fast, with a strange charging movement, out of the clearing and down the path, the wet boughs whipping her. She ran, and he saw nothing but the round wet head, the wet back leaning forward in flight, the rounded buttocks twinkling: a wonderful cowering female nakedness in flight.

She was nearly at the wide riding when he came up and flung his naked arm round her soft, naked-wet middle. She gave a shriek and straightened herself, and the heap of her soft, chill flesh came up against his body. He pressed it all up against him, madly, the heap of soft chilled female flesh that became quickly warm as flame, in contact. The rain streamed on them till they smoked. He gathered her lovely, heavy posteriors one in each hand and pressed them in towards him in a frenzy, quivering motionless in the rain. Then suddenly he tipped her up and fell with her on the path, in the roaring silence of the rain, and short and sharp, he took her, short and sharp and finished, like an animal.

He got up in an instant, wiping the rain from his eyes.

'Come in,' he said, and they started running back to the hut. He ran straight and swift: he didn't like the rain. But she came slower, gathering forget-me-nots and campion and bluebells, running a few steps, and watching him fleeting away from her.

When she came with her flowers, panting to the hut, he had already started a fire, and the twigs were crackling. Her sharp breasts rose and fell, her hair was plastered down with rain, her face was flushed ruddy and her body glistened and trickled. Wide-eyed and breathless, with a small wet head and full, trickling, naïve haunches, she looked another creature.

He took the old sheet and rubbed her down, she standing like a child. Then he rubbed himself, having shut the door of the hut. The fire was blazing up. She ducked her head in the other end of the sheet, and rubbed her wet hair.

'We're drying ourselves together on the same towel, we shall quarrel!' he said.

She looked up for a moment, her hair all odds and ends.

'No!' she said, her eyes wide. 'It's not a towel, it's a sheet.'

And she went on busily rubbing her head, while he busily rubbed his.

Still panting with their exertions, each wrapped in an army blanket, but the front of the body open to the fire, they sat on a log side by side before the blaze, to get quiet. Connie hated the feel of the blanket against her skin. But now the sheet was all wet.

She dropped her blanket and kneeled on the clay hearth, holding her head to the fire, and shaking her hair, to dry it. He watched the beautiful, curving drop of her haunches. That fascinated him today. How it sloped with a rich down-slope, to the heavy roundness of her buttocks! And in between, folded in the secret warmth, the secret entrances!

He stroked her tail with his hand, long and subtly taking in the curves and the globe-fulness.

'Tha's got such a nice tail on thee,' he said, in the throaty, caressive dialect. 'Tha's got the nicest arse of anybody. It's the nicest, nicest woman's arse as is! An' ivry bit of it is woman, woman sure as nuts. Tha'rt not one o' them button-arsed lasses as should be lads, are ter! Tha's got a real soft sloping bottom on thee, as a man loves in 'is guts. It's a bottom as could hold the world up, it is.'

All the while he spoke he exquisitely stroked the rounded tail, till it seemed as if a slippery sort of fire came from it into his hand. And his finger-tips touched the two secret openings to her body, time after time, with a soft little brush of fire.

'An' if tha shits an' if tha pisses, I'm glad. I don't want a woman as couldna shit nor piss.' Connie could not help a sudden snort of astonished laughter, but he went on unmoved. 'Tha'rt real, tha art! Tha'rt real, even a bit of a bitch. Here tha shits an' here tha pisses: an' I lay my hand on 'em both, an' I like thee for it. I like thee for it. Tha's got a proper, woman's arse, proud of itself. It's none ashamed of itself, this isna.'

He laid his hand close and firm over her secret places, in a kind of close greeting.

'I like it,' he said. 'I like it! An' if I only lived ten minutes, an' stroked thy arse an' got to know it, I should reckon I'd lived *one* life, sees ter! Industrial system or not! Here's one o' my lifetimes.'

She turned round and climbed into his lap, clinging to him.

'Kiss me!' she whispered.

And she knew the thought of their separation was latent in both their minds, and at last she was sad.

She sat on his thighs, her head against his breast, and her ivory-gleaming legs loosely apart, the fire glowing unequally upon them. Sitting with his head dropped, he looked at the folds of her body in the fire-glow, and at the fleece of soft brown hair that hung down to a point between her open thighs. He reached to the table behind, and took up her bunch of flowers, still so wet that drops of rain fell on to her.

'Flowers stops out of doors all weathers,' he said. 'They have no houses.'

'Not even a hut!' she murmured.

With quiet fingers he threaded a few forget-me-not flowers in the fine brown fleece of the mount of Venus.

'There!' he said. 'There's forget-me-nots in the right place!'

She looked down at the milky, odd little flowers among the brown maidenhair at the lower tip of her body.

'Doesn't it look pretty!' she said.

'Pretty as life,' he replied.

And he stuck a pink campion-bud among the hair.

'There! That's me where you won't forget me! That's Moses in the bull-rushes.'

'You don't mind, do you, that I'm going away?' she asked wistfully, looking up into his face.

But his face was inscrutable, under the heavy brows. He kept it quite blank.

'You do as you wish,' he said.

And he spoke in good English.

'But I won't go if you don't wish it,' she said, clinging to him.

There was silence. He leaned and put another piece of wood on the fire. The flame glowed on his silent, abstracted face. She waited, but he said nothing.

'Only I thought it would be a good way to begin a break with Clifford. I do want a child. And it would give me a chance to – to—' she resumed.

'To let them think a few lies,' he said.

'Yes, that among other things. Do you want them to think the truth?'

'I don't care what they think.'

'I do! I don't want them handling me with their unpleasant cold minds: not while I'm still at Wragby. They can think what they like when I'm finally gone.'

He was silent.

'But Sir Clifford expects you to come back to him?'

'Oh, I must come back,' she said: and there was silence.

'And would you have a child in Wragby?' he asked.

She closed her arm round his neck.

'If you wouldn't take me away, I should have to,' she said.

'Take you where to?'

'Anywhere! – away! But right away from Wragby.'

'When?'

'Why – when I come back—'

'But what's the good of coming back – doing the thing twice – if you're once gone?' he said.

'Oh, I must come back. I've promised! I've promised so faithfully! Besides, I come back to you, really.'

'To your husband's gamekeeper?'

'I don't see that that matters,' she said.

'No?' he mused awhile. 'And when would you think of going
away again, then, finally? when exactly?'

'Oh, I don't know. I'd come back from Venice – and then we'd
prepare everything.'

'How prepare?'

'Oh – I'd tell Clifford. I'd have to tell him.'

'Would you!'

He remained silent. She put her arms fast round his neck.

'Don't make it difficult for me,' she pleaded.

'Make what difficult?'

'For me to go to Venice – and arrange things.'

A little smile, half a grin, flickered on his face.

'I don't make it difficult,' he said. 'I only want to find out just
what you're after. But you don't really know yourself. You want
to take time: get away and look at it. I don't blame you. I think
you're wise. You may prefer to stay mistress of Wragby. I don't
blame you. I've no Wragbys to offer. In fact, you know what
you'll get out of me. No no, I think you're right! I really do! And
I'm not keen on coming to live on you, being kept by you. There's
that too.'

She felt, somehow, as if he were giving her tit for tat.

'But you want me, don't you?' she asked.

'Do you want me?'

'You know I do. *That's* evident.'

'Quite! And *when* do you want me?'

'You know we can arrange it all when I come back. Now I'm
out of breath with you. I must get calm and clear.'

'Quite! Get calm and clear!'

She was a little offended.

'But you trust me, don't you?' she said.

'Oh, absolutely!'

She heard the mockery in his tone.

'Tell me then,' she said flatly; 'do you think it would be better if I *don't* go to Venice?'

'I'm sure it's better if you *do* go to Venice,' he replied, in the cool, slightly mocking voice.

'You know it's next Thursday?' she said.

'Yes!'

She now began to muse. At last she said:

'And we *shall* know better where we are when I come back, shan't we?'

'Oh surely!'

The curious gulf of silence between them!

'I've been to the lawyer about my divorce,' he said, a little constrainedly.

She gave a slight shudder.

'Have you!' she said. 'And what did he say?'

'He said I ought to have done it before — that may be a difficulty. But since I was in the army — he thinks it'll go through all right. — If only it doesn't bring *her* down on my head!'

'Will she have to know?'

'Yes! She is served with a notice: so is the man she lives with, the co-respondent—'

'Isn't it hateful, all the performances! I suppose I'd have to go through it with Clifford—'

There was a silence.

'And of course,' he said, 'I have to live an exemplary life for the next six or eight months. So if you go to Venice, there's temptation removed for a week or two, at least.'

'Am I temptation!' she said, stroking his face. 'I'm so glad I'm temptation to you! — Don't let's think about it! You frighten me when you start thinking: you roll me out flat. Don't let's think about it. We can think so much when we're apart. That's the whole point! – I've been thinking, I *must* come to you for another night before I go. I must come once more to the cottage. Shall I come on Thursday night?'

'Isn't that when your sister will be there?'

'Yes! But she said we'd start at tea-time. So we could start at tea-time. But she could sleep somewhere else, and I could sleep with you.'

'But then she'd have to know.'

'Oh, I shall tell her. I've more or less told her already. I must talk it all over with Hilda: she's a great help, so sensible.'

He was thinking of her plan.

'So you'd start off from Wragby at tea-time, as if you were going to London? Which way were you going?'

'By Nottingham and Grantham.'

'And then your sister would drop you somewhere, and you'd walk or drive back here? Sounds very risky, to me.'

'Does it? – Well then – well then, Hilda could bring me back. She could sleep at Mansfield, and bring me back here in the evening, and fetch me again in the morning. It's quite easy.'

'And the people who see you?'

'I'll wear goggles and a veil.'

He pondered for some time.

'Well,' he said, 'you please yourself, as usual.'

'But wouldn't it please you?'

'Oh yes! It'd please me all right,' he said, a little grimly. 'I might as well smite while the iron's hot.'

'Do you know what I thought?' she said suddenly. 'It suddenly came to me. You are the "Knight of the Burning Pestle".'

'Ay! And you? Are you the Lady of the Red-hot Mortar?'

'Yes!' she said. 'Yes! You're Sir Pestle and I'm Lady Mortar.'

'All right – then I'm knighted. John Thomas is Sir John, to your Lady Jane.'

'Yes! John Thomas is knighted! I'm my-lady-maidenhair, and you must have flowers too. Yes!'

She threaded two pink campions in the bush of red-gold hair above his penis.

'There!' she said. 'Charming! Charming! Sir John!'

And she pushed a bit of forget-me-not in the dark hair of his breast.

'And you won't forget me *there*, will you?' She kissed him on the breast, and made two bits of forget-me-not lodge one over each nipple, kissing him again.

'Make a calendar of me!' he said. He laughed, and the flowers shook from his breast.

'Wait a bit!' he said.

He rose, and opened the door of the hut. Flossie, lying on the porch, got up and looked at him.

'Ay, it's me!' he said.

The rain had ceased. There was a wet, heavy, perfumed still-ness. Evening was approaching.

He went out and down the little path in the opposite direction from the riding. Connie watched his thin, white figure, and it looked to her like a ghost, an apparition moving away from her. When she could see it no more, her heart sank. She stood in the door of the hut, with a blanket round her, looking into the drenched, motionless silence.

But he was coming back, trotting strangely, and carrying flow-ers. She was a little afraid of him, as if he were not quite human. And when he came near, his eyes looked into hers, but she could not understand the meaning.

He had brought columbines and campions, and new-mown-hay, and oak-tufts and honeysuckle in small bud. He fastened fluffy young oak-sprays round her head, and honeysuckle withes round her breasts, sticking in tufts of bluebells and campion: and in her navel he poised a pink campion flower, and in her maid-enhair were forget-me-nots and wood-ruff.

'That's you in all your glory!' he said. 'Lady Jane, at her wedding with John Thomas.'

And he stuck flowers in the hair of his own body, and wound a bit of creeping-jenny round his penis, and stuck a single bell of a hyacinth in his navel. She watched him with amusement, his odd intentness. And she pushed a campion flower in his moustache, where it stuck, dangling under his nose.

'This is John Thomas marryin' Lady Jane,' he said. 'An' we mun let Constance an' Oliver go their ways. Maybe—' He spread out his hand with a gesture, and then he sneezed, sneezing away the flowers from his nose and his navel. He sneezed again.

'Maybe what?' she said, waiting for him to go on.

He looked at her a little bewildered.

'Eh?' he said.

'Maybe what? Go on with what you were going to say,' she insisted.

'Ay, what *was* I going to say?—'

He had forgotten. And it was one of the disappointments of her life, that he never finished.

A yellow ray of sun shone over the trees.

'Sun!' he said. 'And time you went. Time, my lady, time! What's that as flies without wings, your ladyship? Time! Time!'

He reached for his shirt.

'Say goodnight! to John Thomas,' he said, looking down at his penis. 'He's safe in the arms of creeping-jenny! Not much burning pestle about him just now.'

And he put his thin flannel shirt over his head.

'A man's most dangerous moment,' he said, when his head had emerged, 'is when he's getting into his shirt. Then he puts his head in a bag. That's why I prefer those American shirts, that you put on like a jacket.' She still stood watching him. He stepped into his short drawers, and buttoned them round the waist.

'Look at Jane!' he said. 'In all her blossoms! Who'll put blossoms on you next year, Jinny? Me, or somebody else? "Good-bye my bluebell, farewell to you—!" I hate that song, it's early war days.' He had sat down, and was pulling on his stockings. She still stood unmoving. He laid his hand on the slope of her buttocks. 'Pretty little lady Jane!' he said. 'Perhaps in Venice you'll find a man who'll put jasmine in your maidenhair, and a pomegranate flower in your navel. Poor little lady Jane!'

'Don't say those things!' she said. 'You only say them to hurt me.'

He dropped his head. Then he said, in dialect:

'Ay, maybe I do, maybe I do! Well then, I'll say nowt, an' ha' done wi' it. But tha mun dress thysen, an' go back to thy stately homes of England, how beautiful they stand. Time's up! Time's up for Sir John, an' for little lady Jane! Put thy shimmy on, Lady Chatterley! Tha might be anybody, standin' there be-out even a shimmy, an' a few rags o' flowers. There then, there then, I'll undress thee, tha bob-tailed young throstle—' And he took the leaves from her hair, kissing her damp hair, and the flowers from her breasts, and kissed her breasts, and kissed her navel, and kissed her maidenhair, where he left the flowers threaded. 'They mun stop while they will,' he said. 'So! There tha 'rt bare again, nowt but a bare-arsed lass an' a bit of a lady Jane! Now put thy shimmy on, for tha mun go, or else Lady Chatterley's goin' to be late for dinner, an' where 'ave yer been to my pretty maid!'

She never knew how to answer him when he was in this condition of the vernacular. So she dressed herself and prepared to go a little ignominiously home to Wragby. Or so she felt it: a little ignominiously home.

He would accompany her to the broad riding. His young pheasants were all right under the shelter.

When he and she came out on to the riding, there was Mrs Bolton faltering palely towards them.

'Oh, my Lady, we wondered if anything had happened!'

'No! Nothing has happened.'

Mrs Bolton looked into the man's face, that was smooth and new-looking with love. She met his half-laughing, half-mocking eyes. He always laughed at mischance. But he looked at her kindly.

'Evening, Mrs Bolton! — Your Ladyship will be all right now, so I can leave you. Good-night to your Ladyship! Good-night Mrs Bolton!'

He saluted, and turned away.

AIR

Introduction

The air is unsteady, fearsome and uncontrollable. It is the realm of mind, the idea of the spirit and the world of change. The winds, the clouds, the mist, all atmospheric phenomena, belong to the air. But when we breathe we know that the world is real and that we belong to it. When we take in air, and when we breathe it out, we can feel the very pace of creation. Untouchable, the air can only be felt, or lived. Infinite and invisible, it shapes mountains and creates the waves. It takes up sand and creates the landscapes of reason and madness. When you hear the wind passing through the branches of a tree, you can hear God's voice whispering or roaring his words to you and to the universe. But anger can be found in those winds. St John said, 'The wind bloweth where it listeth, and thou hearest the sound thereof, but canst not tell whence it cometh, and whither it goeth' (John, 3:8). The air is the great sign of the spirit, but it can also be the uncontrolled life of emotions and beliefs abandoned to their own devices. The torment, the tempest or the hurricane are the wages of unconsciousness and passion. Air is linked to blood. Blood, a strange and mysterious fluid, hot and vital . . . Finally, the air allows communication and action, but if it is not tamed it leads to instability and agitation. This ambiguity finds its own path in the texts of this section.

Mandela's letter opens a breach in one of the most unfair political systems of all times, namely apartheid. This letter remains a very clear declaration, a call for freedom and justice. Of course, those two words are in some contexts now out of fashion, but for the people who endured such an unbearable situation those two words were everything. Political action can sometimes touch a kind of universal nerve, and its seeds can give beautiful plants. Far away from politics, the life and fate of Remedios the Beauty in *One Hundred Years of Solitude* transport us to a supernatural America, where the dead smell of strong perfumes and women can fly wrapped in white sheets . . . The parable of Remedios the Beauty reveals the strength of the miraculous and its compelling power of attraction. Stranger yet is *The Strange Case of Dr Jekyll and Mr Hyde*, Robert Louis Stevenson's masterpiece, which tells of the transformation of a scientist into something quite different. The distortion of shape and morals invented by Jekyll bears witness to the unconscious and will given free rein. Like an echo of Wilde's experience, Dr Jekyll imagines a new behaviour, symbolically expressed by a potion. But this one is not the 'potable gold' of the alchemist; it is, rather, a great dissolution of the self and the summoning of unreached parts of the personality. The most impressive illustration of this 'imagination' can be found in the Two Minutes Hate in George Orwell's *Nineteen Eighty-Four*, where people give vent to their innermost fears in a public blast of hate. The reforming revolution turned into something disastrous and people are manipulated and slowly destroyed by Big Brother and his agents. Borges' *Library of Babel* presents itself as a remarkable mirror, despite Borges' own horror of that object. The spectacular structure of the unlikely library throws us into the labyrinth, another favourite theme in the author's work. But the description of the library reveals an obsession with the discovery of the Book, the Book of all books . . . or, better, God's Book. This ultimate journey can be viewed through the insane 'memory' of a great author, recalled in Umberto Eco's *The Name of the Rose*, with 'Jorge de Burgos'. And if air allows travel, it allows, too, losing oneself. And this can be a form of madness.

NELSON MANDELA

from *No Easy Walk to Freedom*

Black Man in a White Man's Court

Mandela was arrested in August of 1962 and put on trial, charged on two counts: inciting African workers to strike; and leaving South Africa without a valid travel document. He turned the trial into a scathing indictment of White domination.

This chapter is an almost complete account of the trial held in Pretoria in the Old Synagogue (converted into a courtroom) where less than two years earlier Mandela and twenty-eight others had been acquitted in the Treason Trial. The trial opened in October 1962. Mandela was sentenced to three years' imprisonment for incitement to strike, and two years' imprisonment on the second charge of leaving South Africa without a valid permit or passport.

Your Worship, I have elected to conduct my own defence. Some time during the progress of these proceedings, I hope to be able to indicate that this case is a trial of the aspirations of the African people, and because of that I thought it proper to conduct my own defence.

I have an application to address to Your Worship. At the outset, I want to make it perfectly clear that the remarks I am going to make are not addressed to Your Worship in his personal capacity, nor are they intended to reflect upon the integrity of the Court.

The point I wish to raise in my argument is based not on personal considerations, but on important questions that go beyond the scope of this present trial. I might also mention that in the course of this application I am frequently going to refer to the White man and the White people. I want at once to make it clear that I am no racialist, and I detest racialism, because I regard it as a barbaric thing, whether it comes from a Black man or from a White man. The terminology that I am going to employ will be compelled on me by the nature of the application I am making.

I want to apply for Your Worship's recusal from this case. I challenge the right of this Court to hear my case on two grounds.

Firstly, I challenge it because I fear that I will not be given a fair and proper trial. Secondly, I consider myself neither legally nor morally bound to obey laws made by a Parliament in which I have no representation.

In a political trial such as this one, which involves a clash of the aspirations of the African people and those of Whites, the country's courts, as presently constituted, cannot be impartial and fair.

In such cases, Whites are interested parties. To have a White judicial officer presiding, however high his esteem, and however strong his sense of fairness and justice, is to make Whites judges in their own case.

It is improper and against the elementary principles of justice to entrust Whites with cases involving the denial by them of basic human rights to the African people.

What sort of justice is this that enables the aggrieved to sit in judgement over those against whom they have laid a charge?

A judiciary controlled entirely by Whites and enforcing laws enacted by a White Parliament in which Africans have no representation – laws which in most cases are passed in the face of unanimous opposition from Africans—

Here the Magistrate interrupted.

*

The Universal Declaration of Human Rights provides that all men are equal before the law and are entitled, without any discrimination, to equal protection of the law.

In May 1951, Dr D. F. Malan, then Prime Minister, told the Union Parliament that this provision of the Declaration applied in this country. Similar statements have been made on numerous occasions in the past by prominent Whites in this country, including judges and magistrates.

But the real truth is that there is in fact no equality before the law whatsoever as far as our people are concerned, and statements to the contrary are definitely incorrect and misleading.

It is true that an African who is charged in a court of law enjoys, on the surface, the same rights and privileges as an accused who is White in so far as the conduct of his trial is concerned. He is governed by the same rules of procedure and evidence as apply to a White accused. But it would be grossly inaccurate to conclude from this fact that an African consequently enjoys equality before the law.

In its proper meaning equality before the law means the right to participate in the making of the laws by which one is governed, a constitution which guarantees democratic rights to all sections of the population, the right to approach the court for protection or relief in the case of the violation of rights guaranteed in the constitution, and the right to take part in the administration of justice as judges, magistrates, attorneys-general, law advisers, and similar positions.

In the absence of these safeguards the phrase 'equality before the law', in so far as it is intended to apply to us, is meaningless and misleading. All the rights and privileges to which I have referred are monopolized by Whites, and we enjoy none of them.

The White man makes all the laws, he drags us before his courts and accuses us, and he sits in judgement over us.

It is fit and proper to raise the question sharply, what is this rigid colour-bar in the administration of justice? Why is it that in this courtroom I face a White magistrate, confronted by a White prosecutor, and escorted into the dock by a White orderly? Can anyone honestly and seriously suggest that in this type of atmosphere the scales of justice are evenly balanced?

Why is it that no African in the history of this country has ever had the honour of being tried by his own kith and kin, by his own flesh and blood?

I will tell Your Worship why: the real purpose of this rigid colour-bar is to ensure that the justice dispensed by the courts should conform to the policy of the country, however much that policy might be in conflict with the norms of justice accepted in judiciaries throughout the civilized world.

I feel oppressed by the atmosphere of White domination that lurks all around in this courtroom. Somehow this atmosphere calls to mind the inhuman injustices caused to my people outside this courtroom by this same White domination.

It reminds me that I am voteless because there is a Parliament in this country that is White-controlled. I am without land because the White minority has taken a lion's share of my country and forced me to occupy poverty-stricken Reserves, over-populated and over-stocked. We are ravaged by starvation and disease . . .

Interruption by the Magistrate.

How can I be expected to believe that this same race discrimination, which has been the cause of so much injustice and suffering right through the years, should now operate here to give me a fair and proper trial? Is there no danger that an African may regard these courts, not as impartial tribunals dispensing justice without fear or favour, but as instruments used by the White man to punish those among us who clamour for deliverance from the fiery furnace of White rule?

I have grave fears that this system of justice may enable the guilty to drag the innocent before the courts. It enables the unjust to prosecute and demand vengeance against the just.

This is the first ground of my objection: that I will not be given a fair and proper trial.

The second ground of my objection is that I consider myself neither morally nor legally obliged to obey laws made by a Parliament in which I am not represented.

That the will of the people is the basis of the authority of government is a principle universally acknowledged as sacred throughout the civilized world, and constitutes the basic foundations of freedom and justice. It is understandable why citizens, who have the vote as well as the right of direct representation in the country's governing bodies, should be morally and legally bound by the laws governing the country.

It would be equally understandable why we, as Africans, should adopt the attitude that we are neither morally nor legally bound to obey laws which we have not made, nor can we be expected to have confidence in courts which enforce such laws.

I am aware that in many cases of this nature in the past, South African courts have upheld the right of the African people to work for democratic changes. Some of our judicial officers have even openly criticized the policy which refuses to acknowledge that all men are born free and equal, and fearlessly condemned the denial of opportunities to our people.

But such exceptions exist in spite of, not because of, the grotesque system of justice that has been built up in this country. These exceptions furnish yet another proof that even among the country's Whites there are honest men whose sense of fairness and justice revolts against the cruelty perpetrated by their own White brothers to our people.

The existence of genuine democratic values among some of the country's Whites in the judiciary, however slender they may be, is welcomed by me. But I have no illusions about the significance of this fact, healthy a sign as it might be. Such honest and upright Whites are few and they have certainly not succeeded in convincing the vast majority of the rest of the White population that White supremacy leads to dangers and disaster.

However, it would be a hopeless commandant who relied for his victories on the few soldiers in the enemy camp who sympathize with his cause. A competent general pins his faith on the superior striking power he commands and on the justness of his cause which he must pursue uncompromisingly to the bitter end.

I hate race discrimination most intensely and in all its manifestations. I have fought it all during my life; I fight it now, and will do so until the end of my days. Even though I now happen to be tried by one whose opinion I hold in high esteem, I detest most violently the set-up that surrounds me here. It makes me feel that I am a Black man in a White man's court. This should not be. I should feel perfectly at ease and at home with the assurance that I am being tried by a fellow South African who does not regard me as an inferior, entitled to a special type of justice.

This is not the type of atmosphere most conducive to feelings of security and confidence in the impartiality of a court.

The Court might reply to this part of my argument by assuring me that it will try my case fairly and without fear or favour, that in deciding whether or not I am guilty of the offence charged by the State, the Court will not be influenced by the colour of my skin or by any other improper motive.

That might well be so. But such a reply would completely miss the point of my argument.

As already indicated, my objection is not directed to Your Worship in his personal capacity, nor is it intended to reflect upon the integrity of the Court. My objection is based upon the fact that our courts, as presently constituted, create grave doubts in the minds of an African accused, whether he will receive a fair and proper trial.

This doubt springs from objective facts relating to the practice of unfair discrimination against the Black man in the constitution of the country's courts. Such doubts cannot be allayed by mere verbal assurances from a presiding officer, however sincere such assurances might be. There is only one way, and one way only, of allaying such doubts, namely, by removing unfair discrimination in judicial appointments. This is my first difficulty.

I have yet another difficulty about similar assurances Your Worship might give. Broadly speaking, Africans and Whites in this country have no common standard of fairness, morality and ethics, and it would be very difficult to determine on my part what standard of fairness and justice Your Worship has in mind.

In their relationship with us, South African Whites regard it as fair and just to pursue policies which have outraged the conscience of mankind and of honest and upright men throughout the civilized world. They suppress our aspirations, bar our way to freedom, and deny us opportunities to promote our moral and material progress, to secure ourselves from fear and want. All the good things of life are reserved for the White folk and we Blacks are expected to be content to nourish our bodies with such pieces of food as drop from the tables of men with White skins. This is the White man's standard of justice and fairness. Herein lies his conception of ethics. Whatever he himself may say in his defence, the White man's moral standards in this country must be judged by the extent to which he has condemned the vast majority of its inhabitants to serfdom and inferiority.

We, on the other hand, regard the struggle against colour discrimination and for the pursuit of freedom and happiness as the highest aspiration of all men. Through bitter experience, we have learnt to regard the White man as a harsh and merciless type of human being whose contempt for our rights, and whose utter indifference to the promotion of our welfare, makes his assurances to us absolutely meaningless and hypocritical.

I have the hope and confidence that Your Worship will not

hear this objection lightly nor regard it as frivolous. I have decided to speak frankly and honestly because the injustice I have referred to contains the seeds of an extremely dangerous situation for our country and people. I make no threat when I say that unless these wrongs are remedied without delay, we might well find that even plain talk before the country's courts is too timid a method to draw the attention of the country to our political demands.

The application for the recusal of the Magistrate was refused.

GABRIEL GARCÍA MÁRQUEZ
from *One Hundred Years of Solitude*

Remedios the Beauty was the only one who was immune to the banana plague. She was becalmed in a magnificent adolescence, more and more impenetrable to formality, more and more indifferent to malice and suspicion, happy in her own world of simple realities. She did not understand why women complicated their lives with corsets and petticoats, so she sewed herself a coarse cassock that she simply put over her and without further difficulties resolved the problem of dress, without taking away the feeling of being naked, which according to her lights was the only decent way to be when at home. They bothered her so much to cut the rain of hair that already reached to her thighs and to make rolls with combs and braids with red ribbons that she simply shaved her head and used the hair to make wigs for the saints. The startling thing about her simplifying instinct was that the more she did away with fashion in a search for comfort and the more she passed over conventions as she obeyed spontaneity, the more disturbing her incredible beauty became and the more provocative she became to men. When the sons of Colonel Aureliano Buendía were in Macondo for the first time, Úrsula remembered that in their veins they bore the same blood as her great-granddaughter and she shuddered with a forgotten fright. 'Keep your eyes wide open,' she warned her. 'With any of them your children will come out with the tail of a pig.' The girl paid such little attention to the warning that she dressed up as a man and rolled around in the sand in order to climb the greased pole, and she was at the point of bringing on a tragedy among the seventeen cousins, who were driven mad by the unbearable spectacle. That was why none of them slept at the house when they visited the town and the four who had stayed lived in rented rooms at Úrsula's insistence. Remedios the Beauty, however, would have died laughing if she had known about that precaution. Until her last moment on earth she was unaware that her irreparable fate as a disturbing woman was a daily disaster. Every time she appeared in the dining room, against Úrsula's orders, she caused a panic of exasperation among the outsiders. It was all too evident that she was completely naked underneath her crude nightshirt and no one could understand that her shaved and perfect skull was not some kind of challenge, and that the boldness with which she uncovered her thighs to cool off was not a criminal provocation, nor was her pleasure when she sucked her fingers after eating. What no member of the family ever knew was that the strangers did not take long to realize that Remedios the Beauty gave off a breath of perturbation, a tormenting breeze that was still perceptible several hours after she had passed by. Men expert in the disturbances of love, experienced all over the world, stated that they had never suffered an anxiety similar to the one produced by the natural smell of Remedios the Beauty. On the porch with the begonias, in the parlour, in any place in the house, it was possible to point out the exact place where she had been and the time that had passed since she had left it. It was a definite, unmistakable trace that no one in the family could distinguish because it had been incorporated into the daily odours for a long time, but it was one that the outsiders identified immediately. They were the only ones, therefore, who understood how the young commander of the guard had died of love and how a gentleman from a faraway land had been plunged into desperation. Unaware of the restless circle in which she moved, of the unbearable state of intimate calamity that she provoked as she passed by, Remedios the Beauty treated the men without the least bit of malice and in the end upset them with her innocent complaisance. When Úrsula succeeded in imposing the command that she eat with Amaranta in the kitchen so that the outsiders would not see her, she felt more comfortable, because, after all, she was beyond all discipline. In reality, it made no difference to her where she ate, and not at regular hours but according to the whims of her appetite. Sometimes she would get up to have lunch at three in the morning, sleep all day long, and she would spend several months with her timetable all in disarray until some casual incident would bring her back into the order of things. When things were going better she would get up at eleven o'clock in the morning and shut herself up until two o'clock, completely nude, in the bathroom, killing scorpions as she came out of her dense and prolonged sleep. Then she would throw water from the cistern over herself with a gourd. It was an act so prolonged, so meticulous, so rich in ceremonial aspects that one who did not know her well would have thought that she was given over to the deserved adoration of her own body. For her, however, that solitary rite lacked all sensuality and was simply a way of passing the time until she was hungry. One day, as she began to bathe herself, a stranger lifted a tile from the roof and was breathless at the tremendous spectacle of her nudity. She saw his desolate eyes through the broken tiles and had no reaction of shame but rather one of alarm.

'Be careful,' she exclaimed. 'You'll fall.'

'I just wanted to see you,' the foreigner murmured.

'Oh, all right,' she said. 'But be careful, those tiles are rotten.'

The stranger's face had a pained expression of stupor and he seemed to be battling silently against his primary instincts so as not to break up the mirage. Remedios the Beauty thought that he was suffering from the fear that the tiles would break and she bathed herself more quickly than usual so that the man would not be in danger. While she was pouring water from the cistern she told him that the roof was in that state because she thought that the bed of leaves had been rotted by the rain and that was what was filling the bathroom with scorpions. The stranger thought that her small talk was a way of covering her complaisance, so that when she began to soap herself he gave into temptation and went a step further.

'Let me soap you,' he murmured.

'Thank you for your good intentions,' she said, 'but my two hands are quite enough.'

'Even if it's just your back,' the foreigner begged.

'That would be silly,' she said. 'People never soap their backs.'

Then, while she was drying herself, the stranger begged her, with his eyes full of tears, to marry him. She answered him sincerely that she would never marry a man who was so simple that he had wasted almost an hour and even went without lunch just to see a woman taking a bath. Finally, when she put on her cassock, the man could not bear the proof that, indeed, she was not wearing anything underneath, as everyone had suspected, and he felt himself marked forever with the white-hot iron of that secret. Then he took two more tiles off in order to drop down into the bathroom.

'It's very high,' she warned him in fright. 'You'll kill yourself!'

The rotten tiles broke with a noise of disaster and the man barely had time to let out a cry of terror as he cracked his skull and was killed outright on the cement floor. The foreigners who heard the noise in the dining room and hastened to remove the body noticed the suffocating odour of Remedios the Beauty on his skin. It was so deep in his body that the cracks in his skull did not give off blood but an amber-coloured oil that was impregnated with that secret perfume, and then they understood that the smell of Remedios the Beauty kept on torturing men beyond death, right down to the dust of their bones. Nevertheless, they did not relate that horrible accident to the other two men who had died because of Remedios the Beauty. A victim was still needed before the outsiders and many of the old inhabitants of Macondo would credit the legend that Remedios Buendía did not give off a breath of love but a fatal emanation. The occasion for the proof of it came some months later on one afternoon when Remedios the Beauty went with a group of girl friends to look at the new plantings. For the girls of Macondo that novel game was reason for laughter and surprises, frights and jokes, and at night they would talk about their walk as if it had been an experience in a dream. Such was the prestige of that silence that Úrsula did not have the heart to take the fun away from Remedios the Beauty, and she let her go one afternoon, providing that she wore a hat and a decent dress. As soon as the group of friends went into the plantings the air became impregnated with a fatal fragrance. The men who were working along the rows felt possessed by a strange fascination, menaced by some invisible danger, and many succumbed to a terrible desire to weep. Remedios the Beauty and her startled friends managed to take refuge in a nearby house just as they were about to be assaulted by a pack of ferocious males. A short time later they were rescued by the four Aurelianos, whose crosses of ash inspired a sacred respect, as if they were caste marks, stamps of invulnerability. Remedios the Beauty did not tell anyone that one of the men, taking advantage of the tumult, had managed to attack her stomach with a hand that was more like the claw of an eagle clinging to the edge of a precipice. She faced the attacker in a kind of instantaneous flash and saw the disconsolate eyes, which remained stamped on her heart like the hot coals of pity. That night the man boasted of his audacity and swaggered over his good luck on the Street of the Turks a few minutes before the kick of a horse crushed his chest and a crowd of outsiders saw him die in the middle of the street, drowned in his own bloody vomiting.

The supposition that Remedios the Beauty possessed powers of death was then borne out by four irrefutable events. Although some men who were easy with their words said that it was worth sacrificing one's life for a night of love with such an arousing woman, the truth was that no one made any effort to do so.

Perhaps, not only to attain her but also to conjure away her dangers, all that was needed was a feeling as primitive and as simple as that of love, but that was the only thing that did not occur to anyone. Úrsula did not worry about her any more. On another occasion, when she had not yet given up the idea of saving her for the world, she had tried to get her interested in basic domestic affairs. 'Men demand much more than you think,' she would tell her enigmatically. 'There's a lot of cooking, a lot of sweeping, a lot of suffering over little things beyond what you think.' She was deceiving herself within, trying to train her for domestic happiness because she was convinced that once his passion was satisfied there would not be a man on the face of the earth capable of tolerating even for a day a negligence that was beyond all understanding. The birth of the latest José Arcadio and her unshakable will to bring him up to be Pope finally caused her to cease worrying about her great-granddaughter. She abandoned her to her fate, trusting that sooner or later a miracle would take place and that in this world of everything there would also be a man with enough sloth to put up with her. For a long time already Amaranta had given up trying to make her into a useful woman. Since those forgotten afternoons when her niece barely had enough interest to turn the crank on the sewing machine, she had reached the conclusion that she was simpleminded. 'We're going to have to raffle you off,' she would tell her, perplexed at the fact that men's words would not penetrate her. Later on, when Úrsula insisted that Remedios the Beauty go to mass with her face covered with a shawl, Amaranta thought that a mysterious recourse like that would turn out to be so provoking that soon a man would come who would be intrigued enough to search out patiently for the weak point of her heart. But when she saw the stupid way in which she rejected a pretender who for many reasons was more desirable than a prince, she gave up all hope. Fernanda did not even make any attempt to understand her. When she saw Remedios the Beauty dressed as a queen at the bloody carnival she thought that she was an extraordinary creature. But when she saw her eating with her hands, incapable of giving an answer that was not a miracle of simplemindedness, the only thing that she lamented was the fact that the idiots in the family lived so long. In spite of the fact that Colonel Aureliano Buendía kept on believing and repeating that Remedios the Beauty was in reality the most lucid being that he had ever known and that she showed it at every moment with her startling ability to put things over on everyone, they let her go her own way. Remedios the Beauty stayed there wandering through the desert of solitude, bearing no cross on her back, maturing in her dreams without nightmares, her interminable baths, her unscheduled meals, her deep and prolonged silences that had no memory until one afternoon in March, when Fernanda wanted to fold her brabant sheets in the garden and asked the women in the house for help. She had just begun when Amaranta noticed that Remedios the Beauty was covered all over by an intense paleness.

'Don't you feel well?' she asked her.

Remedios the Beauty, who was clutching the sheet by the other end, gave a pitying smile.

'Quite the opposite,' she said, 'I never felt better.'

She had just finished saying it when Fernanda felt a delicate wind of light pull the sheets out of her hands and open them up wide. Amaranta felt a mysterious trembling in the lace on her petticoats and she tried to grasp the sheet so that she would not fall down at the instant in which Remedios the Beauty began to rise. Úrsula, almost blind at the time, was the only person who was sufficiently calm to identify the nature of that determined wind and she left the sheets to the mercy of the light as she watched Remedios the Beauty waving good-bye in the midst of the flapping sheets that rose up with her, abandoning with her the environment of beetles and dahlias and passing through the air with her as four o'clock in the afternoon came to an end, and they were lost forever with her in the upper atmosphere where not even the highest-flying birds of memory could reach her.

The outsiders, of course, thought that Remedios the Beauty had finally succumbed to her irrevocable fate of a queen bee and that her family was trying to save her honour with that tale of levitation. Fernanda, burning with envy, finally accepted the miracle, and for a long time she kept on praying to God to send her back her sheets. Most people believed in the miracle and they even lighted candles and celebrated novenas.

ROBERT LOUIS STEVENSON

from *The Strange Case of Dr Jekyll and Mr Hyde*

Henry Jekyll's Full Statement of the Case

I was born in the year 18— to a large fortune, endowed besides with excellent parts, inclined by nature to industry, fond of the respect of the wise and good among my fellow-men, and thus, as might have been supposed, with every guarantee of an honourable and distinguished future. And indeed the worst of my faults was a certain impatient gaiety of disposition, such as has made the happiness of many, but such as I found it hard to reconcile with my imperious desire to carry my head high, and wear a more than commonly grave countenance before the public. Hence it came about that I concealed my pleasures; and that when I reached years of reflection, and began to look round me and take stock of my progress and position in the world, I stood already committed to a profound duplicity of life. Many a man would have even blazoned such irregularities as I was guilty of; but from the high views that I had set before me, I regarded and hid them with an almost morbid sense of shame. It was thus rather the exacting nature of my aspirations than any particular degradation in my faults, that made me what I was and, with even a deeper trench than in the majority of men, severed in me those provinces of good and ill which divide and compound man's dual nature. In this case, I was driven to reflect deeply and inveterately on that hard law of life, which lies at the root of religion and is one of the most plentiful springs of distress. Though so profound a double-dealer, I was in no sense a hypocrite; both sides of me were in dead earnest; I was no more myself when I laid aside restraint and plunged in shame, than when I laboured, in the eye of day, at the furtherance of knowledge or the relief of sorrow and suffering. And it chanced that the direction of my scientific studies, which led wholly towards the mystic and the transcendental, reacted and shed a strong light on this consciousness of the perennial war among my members. With every day, and from both sides of my intelligence, the moral and the intellectual, I thus drew steadily nearer to that truth, by whose partial discovery I have been doomed to such a dreadful shipwreck: that man is not truly one, but truly two. I say two, because the state of my own knowledge does not pass beyond that point. Others will follow, others will outstrip me on the same lines; and I hazard the guess that man will be ultimately known for a mere polity of multifarious, incongruous and independent denizens. I for my part, from the nature of my life, advanced infallibly in one direction and in one direction only. It was on the moral side, and in my own person, that I learned to recognize the thorough and primitive duality of man; I saw that, of the two natures that contended in the field of my consciousness, even if I could rightly be said to be either, it was only because I was radically both; and from an early date, even before the course of my scientific discoveries had begun to suggest the most naked possibility of such a miracle, I had learned to dwell with pleasure, as a beloved daydream, on the thought of the separation of these elements. If each, I told myself, could but be housed in separate identities, life would be relieved of all that was unbearable; the unjust might go his way, delivered from the aspirations and remorse of his more upright twin; and the just could walk steadfastly and securely on his upward path, doing the good things in which he found his pleasure, and no longer exposed to disgrace and penitence by the hands of this extraneous evil. It was the curse of mankind that these incongruous faggots were thus bound together – that in the agonized womb of consciousness, these polar twins should be continuously struggling. How, then, were they dissociated?

I was so far in my reflections when, as I have said, a side light began to shine upon the subject from the laboratory table. I began to perceive more deeply than it has ever yet been stated, the trembling immateriality, the mist-like transience, of this seemingly so solid body in which we walk attired. Certain agents I found to have the power to shake and to pluck back that fleshly vestment, even as a wind might toss the curtains of a pavilion. For two good reasons, I will not enter deeply into this scientific branch of my confession. First, because I have been made to learn that the doom and burden of our life is bound for ever on man's shoulders, and when the attempt is made to cast it off, it but returns upon us with more unfamiliar and more awful pressure. Second, because as my narrative will make alas! too evident, my discoveries were incomplete. Enough, then, that I not only recognized my natural body for the mere aura and effulgence of certain of the powers that made up my spirit, but managed to compound a drug by which these powers should be dethroned from their supremacy, and a second form and countenance substituted, none the less natural to me because they were the expression, and bore the stamp, of lower elements in my soul.

I hesitated long before I put this theory to the test of practice. I knew well that I risked death; for any drug that so potently controlled and shook the very fortress of identity, might by the least scruple of an overdose or at the least inopportunity in the moment of exhibition, utterly blot out that immaterial tabernacle which I looked to it to change. But the temptation of a discovery so singular and profound, at last overcame the suggestions of alarm. I had long since prepared my tincture; I purchased at once, from a firm of wholesale chemists, a large quantity of a particular salt which I knew, from my experiments, to be the last ingredient required; and late one accursed night, I compounded the elements, watched them boil and smoke together in the glass, and when the ebullition had subsided, with a strong glow of courage, drank off the potion.

The most racking pangs succeeded: a grinding in the bones, deadly nausea, and a horror of the spirit that cannot be exceeded at the hour of birth or death. Then these agonies began swiftly to subside, and I came to myself as if out of a great sickness. There was something strange in my sensations, something indescribably new and, from its very novelty, incredibly sweet. I felt younger, lighter, happier in body; within I was conscious of a heady reck-lessness, a current of disordered sensual images running like a mill race in my fancy, a solution of the bonds of obligation, an unknown but not an innocent freedom of the soul. I knew myself, at the first breath of this new life, to be more wicked, tenfold more wicked, sold a slave to my original evil; and the thought, in that moment, braced and delighted me like wine. I stretched out my hands, exulting in the freshness of these sensations; and in the act, I was suddenly aware that I had lost in stature.

There was no mirror, at that date, in my room; that which stands beside me as I write, was brought there later on and for the very purpose of these transformations. The night, however, was far gone into the morning – the morning, black as it was, was nearly ripe for the conception of the day – the inmates of my house were locked in the most rigorous hours of slumber; and I determined, flushed as I was with hope and triumph, to venture in my new shape as far as to my bedroom. I crossed the yard, wherein the constellations looked down upon me, I could have thought, with wonder, the first creature of that sort that their unsleeping vigilance had yet disclosed to them; I stole through the corridors, a stranger in my own house; and coming to my room, I saw for the first time the appearance of Edward Hyde.

I must here speak by theory alone, saying not that which I know, but that which I suppose to be most probable. The evil side of my nature, to which I had now transferred the stamping efficacy, was less robust and less developed than the good which I had just deposed. Again, in the course of my life, which had been, after all, nine tenths a life of effort, virtue and control, it had been much less exercised and much less exhausted. And hence, as I think, it came about that Edward Hyde was so much smaller, slighter and younger than Henry Jekyll. Even as good shone upon the countenance of the one, evil was written broadly and plainly on the face of the other. Evil besides (which I must still believe to be the lethal side of man) had left on that body an imprint of deformity and decay. And yet when I looked upon that ugly idol in the glass, I was conscious of no repugnance, rather of a leap of welcome. This, too, was myself. It seemed natural and human. In my eyes it bore a livelier image of the spirit, it seemed more express and single, than the imperfect and divided countenance I had been hitherto accustomed to call mine. And in so far I was doubtless right. I have observed that when I wore the semblance of Edward Hyde, none could come near to me at first without a visible misgiving of the flesh. This, as I take it, was because all human beings, as we meet them, are commingled out of good and evil: and Edward Hyde, alone in the ranks of mankind, was pure evil.

I lingered but a moment at the mirror: the second and conclusive experiment had yet to be attempted; it yet remained to be seen if I had lost my identity beyond redemption and must flee before daylight from a house that was no longer mine; and hurrying back to my cabinet, I once more prepared and drank the cup, once more suffered the pangs of dissolution, and came to myself once more with the character, the stature and the face of Henry Jekyll.

That night I had come to the fatal cross roads. Had I approached my discovery in a more noble spirit, had I risked the experiment while under the empire of generous or pious aspirations, all must have been otherwise, and from these agonies of death and birth, I had come forth an angel instead of a fiend. The drug had no discriminating action; it was neither diabolical nor divine; it but shook the doors of the prisonhouse of my disposition; and like the captives of Philippi, that which stood within ran forth. At that time my virtue slumbered; my evil, kept awake by ambition, was alert and swift to seize the occasion; and the thing that was projected was Edward Hyde. Hence, although I had now two characters as well as two appearances, one was wholly evil, and the other was still the old Henry Jekyll, that incongruous compound of whose reformation and improvement I had already learned to despair. The movement was thus wholly towards the worse.

Even at that time, I had not yet conquered my aversion to the dryness of a life of study. I would still be merrily disposed at times; and as my pleasures were (to say the least) undignified, and I was not only well known and highly considered, but growing towards the elderly man, this incoherency of my life was daily growing more unwelcome. It was on this side that my new power tempted me until I fell in slavery. I had but to drink the cup, to doff at once the body of the noted professor, and to assume, like a thick cloak, that of Edward Hyde. I smiled at the notion; it seemed to me at the time to be humorous; and I made my preparations with the most studious care. I took and furnished that house in Soho, to which Hyde was tracked by the police; and engaged as housekeeper a creature whom I well knew to be silent and unscrupulous. On the other side, I announced to my servants that a Mr Hyde (whom I described) was to have full liberty and power about my house in the square; and to parry mishaps, I even called and made myself a familiar object, in my second character. I next drew up that will to which you so much objected; so that if anything befell me in the person of Doctor Jekyll, I could enter on that of Edward Hyde without pecuniary loss. And thus fortified, as I supposed, on every side, I began to profit by the strange immunities of my position.

Men have before hired bravos to transact their crimes, while their own person and reputation sat under shelter. I was the first that ever did so for his pleasures. I was the first that could thus plod in the public eye with a load of genial respectability, and in a moment, like a schoolboy, strip off these lendings and spring headlong into the sea of liberty. But for me, in my impenetrable mantle, the safety was complete. Think of it – I did not even exist! Let me but escape into my laboratory door, give me but a second or two to mix and swallow the draught that I had always standing ready; and whatever he had done, Edward Hyde would pass away like the stain of breath upon a mirror; and there in his stead, quietly at home, trimming the midnight lamp in his study, a man who could afford to laugh at suspicion, would be Henry Jekyll.

The pleasures which I made haste to seek in my disguise were, as I have said, undignified; I would scarce use a harder term. But in the hands of Edward Hyde, they soon began to turn towards the monstrous. When I would come back from these excursions, I was often plunged into a kind of wonder at my vicarious depravity. This familiar that I called out of my own soul, and sent forth alone to do his good pleasure, was a being inherently malign and villainous; his every act and thought centred on self; drinking pleasure with bestial avidity from any degree of torture to another; relentless like a man of stone. Henry Jekyll stood at times aghast before the acts of Edward Hyde; but the situation was apart from ordinary laws, and insidiously relaxed the grasp of conscience. It was Hyde, after all, and Hyde alone, that was guilty. Jekyll was no worse; he woke again to his good qualities seemingly unimpaired; he would even make haste, where it was possible, to undo the evil done by Hyde. And thus his conscience slumbered.

GEORGE ORWELL

from *Nineteen Eighty-Four*

Winston stopped writing, partly because he was suffering from cramp. He did not know what had made him pour out this stream of rubbish. But the curious thing was that while he was doing so a totally different memory had clarified itself in his mind, to the point where he almost felt equal to writing it down. It was, he now realized, because of this other incident that he had suddenly decided to come home and begin the diary today.

It had happened that morning at the Ministry, if anything so nebulous could be said to happen.

It was nearly eleven hundred, and in the Records Department, where Winston worked, they were dragging the chairs out of the cubicles and grouping them in the centre of the hall, opposite the big telescreen, in preparation for the Two Minutes Hate. Winston was just taking his place in one of the middle rows when two people whom he knew by sight, but had never spoken to, came unexpectedly into the room. One of them was a girl whom he often passed in the corridors. He did not know her name, but he knew that she worked in the Fiction Department. Presumably – since he had sometimes seen her with oily hands and carrying a spanner – she had some mechanical job on one of the novel-writing machines. She was a bold-looking girl, of about twenty-seven, with thick dark hair, a freckled face and swift, athletic movements. A narrow scarlet sash, emblem of the Junior Anti-Sex League, was wound several times round the waist of her overalls, just tightly enough to bring out the shapeliness of her hips. Winston had disliked her from the very first moment of seeing her. He knew the reason. It was because of the atmosphere of hockey-fields and cold baths and community hikes and general clean-mindedness which she managed to carry about with her. He disliked nearly all women, and especially the young and pretty ones. It was always the women, and above all the young ones, who were the most bigoted adherents of the Party, the swallowers of slogans, the amateur spies and nosers-out of unorthodoxy. But this particular girl gave him the impression of being more dangerous than most. Once when they passed in the corridor she had given him a quick sidelong glance which seemed to pierce right into him and for a moment had filled him with black terror. The idea had even crossed his mind that she might be an agent of the Thought Police. That, it was true, was very unlikely. Still, he continued to feel a peculiar uneasiness, which had fear mixed up in it as well as hostility, whenever she was anywhere near him.

The other person was a man named O'Brien, a member of the Inner Party and holder of some post so important and remote that Winston had only a dim idea of its nature. A momentary hush passed over the group of people round the chairs as they saw the black overalls of an Inner Party member approaching. O'Brien was a large, burly man with a thick neck and a coarse, humorous, brutal face. In spite of his formidable appearance he had a certain charm of manner. He had a trick of re-settling his spectacles on his nose which was curiously disarming – in some indefinable way, curiously civilized. It was a gesture which, if anyone had still thought in such terms, might have recalled an eighteenth-century nobleman offering his snuff-box. Winston had seen O'Brien perhaps a dozen times in almost as many years. He felt deeply drawn to him, and not solely because he was intrigued by the contrast between O'Brien's urbane manner and his prizefighter's physique. Much more it was because of a secretly held belief – or perhaps not even a belief, merely a hope

– that O'Brien's political orthodoxy was not perfect. Something in his face suggested it irresistibly. And again, perhaps it was not even unorthodoxy that was written in his face, but simply intelligence. But at any rate he had the appearance of being a person that you could talk to, if somehow you could cheat the telescreen and get him alone. Winston had never made the smallest effort to verify this guess: indeed, there was no way of doing so. At this moment O'Brien glanced at his wristwatch, saw that it was nearly eleven hundred and evidently decided to stay in the Records Department until the Two Minutes Hate was over. He took a chair in the same row as Winston, a couple of places away. A small, sandy-haired woman who worked in the next cubicle to Winston was between them. The girl with dark hair was sitting immediately behind.

The next moment a hideous, grinding screech, as of some monstrous machine running without oil, burst from the big telescreen at the end of the room. It was a noise that set one's teeth on edge and bristled the hair at the back of one's neck. The Hate had started.

As usual, the face of Emmanuel Goldstein, the Enemy of the People, had flashed onto the screen. There were hisses here and there among the audience. The little sandy-haired woman gave a squeak of mingled fear and disgust. Goldstein was the renegade and backslider who once, long ago (how long ago, nobody quite remembered), had been one of the leading figures of the Party, almost on a level with Big Brother himself, and then had engaged in counter-revolutionary activities, had been condemned to death and had mysteriously escaped and disappeared. The programmes of the Two Minutes Hate varied from day to day, but there was none in which Goldstein was not the principal figure. He was the primal traitor, the earliest defiler of the Party's purity. All subsequent crimes against the Party, all treacheries, acts of sabotage, heresies, deviations, sprang directly out of his teaching. Somewhere or other he was still alive and hatching his conspiracies:

perhaps somewhere beyond the sea, under the protection of his foreign paymasters, perhaps even – so it was occasionally rumoured – in some hiding-place in Oceania itself.

Winston's diaphragm was constricted. He could never see the face of Goldstein without a painful mixture of emotions. It was a lean Jewish face, with a great fuzzy aureole of white hair and a small goatee beard – a clever face, and yet somehow inherently despicable, with a kind of senile silliness in the long thin nose near the end of which a pair of spectacles was perched. It resembled the face of a sheep, and the voice, too, had a sheeplike quality. Goldstein was delivering his usual venomous attack upon the doctrines of the Party – an attack so exaggerated and perverse that a child should have been able to see through it, and yet just plausible enough to fill one with an alarmed feeling that other people, less level-headed than oneself, might be taken in by it. He was abusing Big Brother, he was denouncing the dictatorship of the Party, he was demanding the immediate conclusion of peace with Eurasia, he was advocating freedom of speech, freedom of the press, freedom of assembly, freedom of thought, he was crying hysterically that the revolution had been betrayed – and all this in rapid polysyllabic speech which was a sort of parody of the habitual style of the orators of the Party, and even contained Newspeak words: more Newspeak words, indeed, than any Party member would normally use in real life. And all the while, lest one should be in any doubt as to the reality which Goldstein's specious claptrap covered, behind his head on the telescreen there marched the endless columns of the Eurasian army – row after row of solid-looking men with expressionless Asiatic faces, who swam up to the surface of the screen and vanished, to be replaced by others exactly similar. The dull rhythmic tramp of the soldiers' boots formed the background to Goldstein's bleating voice.

Before the Hate had proceeded for thirty seconds, uncontrollable exclamations of rage were breaking out from half the people in the room. The self-satisfied sheeplike face on the screen, and the terrifying power of the Eurasian army behind it, were too much to be borne: besides, the sight or even the thought of Goldstein produced fear and anger automatically. He was an object of hatred more constant than either Eurasia or Eastasia, since when Oceania was at war with one of these powers it was generally at peace with the other. But what was strange was that although Goldstein was hated and despised by everybody, although every day, and a thousand times a day, on platforms, on the telescreen, in newspapers, in books, his theories were refuted, smashed, ridiculed, held up to the general gaze for the pitiful rubbish that they were – in spite of all this, his influence never seemed to grow less. Always there were fresh dupes waiting to be seduced by him. A day never passed when spies and saboteurs acting under his directions were not unmasked by the Thought Police. He was the commander of a vast shadowy army, an underground network of conspirators dedicated to the overthrow of the State. The Brotherhood, its name was supposed to be. There were also whispered stories of a terrible book, a compendium of all the heresies, of which Goldstein was the author and which circulated clandestinely here and there. It was a book without a title. People referred to it, if at all, simply as *the book*. But one knew of such things only through vague rumours. Neither the Brotherhood nor *the book* was a subject that any ordinary Party member would mention if there was a way of avoiding it.

In its second minute the Hate rose to a frenzy. People were leaping up and down in their places and shouting at the tops of their voices in an effort to drown the maddening bleating voice that came from the screen. The little sandy-haired woman had turned bright pink, and her mouth was opening and shutting like that of a landed fish. Even O'Brien's heavy face was flushed. He was sitting very straight in his chair, his powerful chest swelling and quivering as though he were standing up to the assault of a wave. The dark-haired girl behind Winston had begun crying out 'Swine! Swine! Swine!', and suddenly she picked up a heavy Newspeak dictionary and flung it at the screen. It struck Goldstein's nose and bounced off: the voice continued inexorably. In a lucid moment Winston found that he was shouting with the others and kicking his heel violently against the rung of his chair. The horrible thing about the Two Minutes Hate was not that one was obliged to act a part, but that it was impossible to avoid joining in. Within thirty seconds any pretence was always unnecessary. A hideous ecstasy of fear and vindictiveness, a desire to kill, to torture, to smash faces in with a sledgehammer, seemed to flow through the whole group of people like an electric current, turning one even against one's will into a grimacing, screaming lunatic. And yet the rage that one felt was an abstract, undirected emotion which could be switched from one object to another like the flame of a blowlamp. Thus, at one moment Winston's hatred was not turned against Goldstein at all, but, on the contrary, against Big Brother, the Party and the Thought Police; and at such moments his heart went out to the lonely, derided heretic on the screen, sole guardian of truth and sanity in a world of lies. And yet the very next instant he was at one with the people about him, and all that was said of Goldstein seemed to him to be true. At those moments his secret loathing of Big Brother changed into adoration, and Big Brother seemed to tower up, an invincible, fearless protector, standing like a rock against the hordes of Asia, and Goldstein, in spite of his isolation, his helplessness and the doubt that hung about his very existence, seemed like some sinister enchanter, capable by the mere power of his voice of wrecking the structure of civilization.

It was even possible, at moments, to switch one's hatred this way or that by a voluntary act. Suddenly, by the sort of violent effort with which one wrenches one's head away from the pillow in a nightmare, Winston succeeded in transferring his hatred from the face on the screen to the dark-haired girl behind him.

Vivid, beautiful hallucinations flashed through his mind. He would flog her to death with a rubber truncheon. He would tie her naked to a stake and shoot her full of arrows like Saint Sebastian. He would ravish her and cut her throat at the moment of climax. Better than before, moreover, he realized *why* it was that he hated her. He hated her because she was young and pretty and sexless, because he wanted to go to bed with her and would never do so, because round her sweet supple waist, which seemed to ask you to encircle it with your arm, there was only the odious scarlet sash, aggressive symbol of chastity.

The Hate rose to its climax. The voice of Goldstein had become an actual sheep's bleat, and for an instant the face changed into that of a sheep. Then the sheep-face melted into the figure of a Eurasian soldier who seemed to be advancing, huge and terrible, his sub-machine-gun roaring, and seeming to spring out of the surface of the screen, so that some of the people in the front row actually flinched backwards in their seats. But in the same moment, drawing a deep sigh of relief from everybody, the hostile figure melted into the face of Big Brother, black-haired, black-moustachio'd, full of power and mysterious calm, and so vast that it almost filled up the screen. Nobody heard what Big Brother was saying. It was merely a few words of encouragement, the sort of words that are uttered in the din of battle, not distinguishable individually but restoring confidence by the fact of being spoken. Then the face of Big Brother faded away again and instead the three slogans of the Party stood out in bold capitals:

WAR IS PEACE
FREEDOM IS SLAVERY
IGNORANCE IS STRENGTH.

But the face of Big Brother seemed to persist for several seconds on the screen, as though the impact that it had made on everyone's eyeballs was too vivid to wear off immediately. The little sandy-haired woman had flung herself forward over the back of the chair in front of her. With a tremulous murmur that sounded like 'My Saviour!' she extended her arms towards the screen. Then she buried her face in her hands. It was apparent that she was uttering a prayer.

At this moment the entire group of people broke into a deep, slow, rhythmical chant of 'B-B! . . . B-B! . . . B-B!' – over and over again, very slowly, with a long pause between the first 'B' and the second – a heavy, murmurous sound, somehow curiously savage, in the background of which one seemed to hear the stamp of naked feet and the throbbing of tom-toms. For perhaps as much as thirty seconds they kept it up. It was a refrain that was often heard in moments of overwhelming emotion. Partly it was a sort of hymn to the wisdom and majesty of Big Brother, but still more it was an act of self-hypnosis, a deliberate drowning of consciousness by means of rhythmic noise. Winston's entrails seemed to grow cold. In the Two Minutes Hate he could not help sharing in the general delirium, but this sub-human chanting of 'B-B! . . . B-B!' always filled him with horror. Of course he chanted with the rest: it was impossible to do otherwise. To dissemble your feelings, to control your face, to do what every-one else was doing, was an instinctive reaction. But there was a space of a couple of seconds during which the expression in his eyes might conceivably have betrayed him. And it was exactly at this moment that the significant thing happened – if, indeed, it did happen.

Momentarily he caught O'Brien's eye. O'Brien had stood up. He had taken off his spectacles and was in the act of re-settling them on his nose with his characteristic gesture. But there was a fraction of a second when their eyes met, and for as long as it took to happen Winston knew – yes, he *knew*! – that O'Brien was thinking the same thing as himself. An unmistakable message had passed. It was as though their two minds had opened and the thoughts were flowing from one into the other through their eyes.

'I am with you,' O'Brien seemed to be saying to him. 'I know precisely what you are feeling. I know all about your contempt, your hatred, your disgust. But don't worry, I am on your side!' And then the flash of intelligence was gone, and O'Brien's face was as inscrutable as everybody else's.

That was all, and he was already uncertain whether it had happened. Such incidents never had any sequel. All that they did was to keep alive in him the belief, or hope, that others besides himself were the enemies of the Party.

JORGE LUIS BORGES

from *Fictions*

The Library of Babel

By this art you may contemplate the variation of the 23 letters . . .
Anatomy of Melancholy Pt 2, Sec. II, Mem. IV

The universe (which others call the Library) is composed of an
indefinite, perhaps infinite number of hexagonal galleries. In the
centre of each gallery is a ventilation shaft, bounded by a low
railing. From any hexagon one can see the floors above and below
– one after another, endlessly. The arrangement of the galleries
is always the same: Twenty bookshelves, five to each side, line
four of the hexagon's six sides; the height of the bookshelves,
floor to ceiling, is hardly greater than the height of a normal
librarian. One of the hexagon's free sides opens on to a narrow
sort of vestibule, which in turn opens on to another gallery, identical to the first – identical in fact to all. To the left and right of
the vestibule are two tiny compartments. One is for sleeping,
upright; the other, for satisfying one's physical necessities.
Through this space, too, there passes a spiral staircase, which
winds upward and downward into the remotest distance. In the
vestibule there is a mirror, which faithfully duplicates appearances. Men often infer from this mirror that the Library is not
infinite – if it were, what need would there be for that illusory
replication? I prefer to dream that burnished surfaces are a figu-
ration and promise of the infinite . . . Light is provided by certain

spherical fruits that bear the name 'bulbs'. There are two of these bulbs in each hexagon, set crosswise. The light they give is insufficient, and unceasing.

Like all the men of the Library, in my younger days I travelled; I have journeyed in quest of a book, perhaps the catalogue of catalogues. Now that my eyes can hardly make out what I myself have written, I am preparing to die, a few leagues from the hexagon where I was born. When I am dead, compassionate hands will throw me over the railing; my tomb will be the unfathomable air, my body will sink for ages, and will decay and dissolve in the wind engendered by my fall, which shall be infinite. I declare that the Library is endless. Idealists argue that the hexagonal rooms are the necessary shape of absolute space, or at least of our *perception* of space. They argue that a triangular or pentagonal chamber is inconceivable. (Mystics claim that their ecstasies reveal to them a circular chamber containing an enormous circular book with a continuous spine that goes completely around the walls. But their testimony is suspect, their words obscure. That cyclical book is God.) Let it suffice for the moment that I repeat the classic dictum: *The Library is a sphere whose exact centre is any hexagon and whose circumference is unattainable.*

Each wall of each hexagon is furnished with five bookshelves; each bookshelf holds thirty-two books identical in format; each book contains four hundred and ten pages; each page, forty lines; each line, approximately eighty black letters. There are also letters on the front cover of each book; those letters neither indicate nor prefigure what the pages inside will say. I am aware that that lack of correspondence once struck men as mysterious. Before summarizing the solution of the mystery (whose discovery, in spite of its tragic consequences, is perhaps the most important event in all history), I wish to recall a few axioms.

First: *The Library has existed* ab æternitate. That truth, whose immediate corollary is the future eternity of the world, no rational mind can doubt. Man, the imperfect librarian, may be the work of chance or of malevolent demiurges; the universe, with its elegant appointments – its bookshelves, its enigmatic books, its indefatigable staircases for the traveller, and its water closets for the seated librarian – can only be the handiwork of a god. In order to grasp the distance that separates the human and the divine, one has only to compare these crude trembling symbols which my fallible hand scrawls on the cover of a book with the organic letters inside – neat, delicate, deep black and inimitably symmetrical.

Second: *There are twenty-five orthographic symbols.** That discovery enabled mankind, three hundred years ago, to formulate a general theory of the Library and thereby satisfactorily solve the riddle that no conjecture had been able to divine – the formless and chaotic nature of virtually all books. One book, which my father once saw in a hexagon in circuit 15–94, consisted of the letters M C V perversely repeated from the first line to the last. Another (much consulted in this zone) is a mere labyrinth of letters whose penultimate page contains the phrase *O Time thy pyramids*. This much is known: For every rational line or forthright statement there are leagues of senseless cacophony, verbal nonsense and incoherency. (I know of one semibarbarous zone whose librarians repudiate the 'vain and superstitious habit' of trying to find sense in books, equating such a quest with attempting to find meaning in dreams or in the chaotic lines of the palm of one's hand . . . They will acknowledge that the inventors of writing imitated the twenty-five natural symbols, but contend that that adoption was fortuitous, coincidental, and that books in themselves have no meaning. That argument, as we shall see, is not entirely fallacious.)

For many years it was believed that those impenetrable books were in ancient or far-distant languages. It is true that the most ancient peoples, the first librarians, employed a language quite

* The original manuscript has neither numbers nor capital letters; punctuation is limited to the comma and the period. Those two marks, the space and the twenty-two letters of the alphabet are the twenty-five sufficient symbols that our unknown author is referring to. [Ed. note.]

different from the one we speak today; it is true that a few miles to the right, our language devolves into dialect and that ninety floors above, it becomes incomprehensible. All of that, I repeat, is true – but four hundred and ten pages of unvarying M C Vs cannot belong to any language, however dialectal or primitive it may be. Some have suggested that each letter influences the next, and that the value of M C V on page 71, line 3, is not the value of the same series on another line of another page, but that vague thesis has not met with any great acceptance. Others have mentioned the possibility of codes; that conjecture has been universally accepted, though not in the sense in which its originators formulated it.

Some five hundred years ago, the chief of one of the upper hexagons* came across a book as jumbled as all the others, but containing almost two pages of homogeneous lines. He showed his find to a travelling decipherer, who told him that the lines were written in Portuguese; others said it was Yiddish. Within the century experts had determined what the language actually was: a Samoyed-Lithuanian dialect of Guaraní, with inflections from classical Arabic. The content was also determined: the rudiments of combinatory analysis, illustrated with examples of endlessly repeating variations. Those examples allowed a librarian of genius to discover the fundamental law of the Library. This philosopher observed that all books, however different from one another they might be, consist of identical elements: the space, the period, the comma and the twenty-two letters of the alphabet. He also posited a fact which all travellers have since confirmed: *In all the Library, there are no two identical books*. From those incontrovertible premises, the librarian deduced that the Library is 'total' – perfect, complete and whole – and that its bookshelves contain all possible combinations of the twenty-two

---

* In earlier times, there was one man for every three hexagons. Suicide and diseases of the lung have played havoc with that proportion. An unspeakably melancholy memory: I have sometimes travelled for nights on end, down corridors and polished staircases, without coming across a single librarian.

orthographic symbols (a number which, though unimaginably vast, is not infinite) – that is, all that is able to be expressed, in every language. *All* – the detailed history of the future, the auto-biographies of the archangels, the faithful catalogue of the Library, thousands and thousands of false catalogues, the proof of the falsity of those false catalogues, a proof of the falsity of the *true* catalogue, the gnostic gospel of Basilides, the commen-tary upon that gospel, the commentary on the commentary on that gospel, the true story of your death, the translation of every book into every language, the interpolations of every book into all books, the treatise Bede could have written (but did not) on the mythology of the Saxon people, the lost books of Tacitus.

When it was announced that the Library contained all books, the first reaction was unbounded joy. All men felt themselves the possessors of an intact and secret treasure. There was no personal problem, no world problem, whose eloquent solution did not exist – somewhere in some hexagon. The universe was justified; the universe suddenly became congruent with the unlimited width and breadth of humankind's hope. At that period there was much talk of The Vindications – books of *apologiæ* and prophecies that would vindicate for all time the actions of every person in the universe and that held wondrous arcana for men's futures. Thousands of greedy individuals abandoned their sweet native hexagons and rushed downstairs, upstairs, spurred by the vain desire to find their Vindication. These pilgrims squabbled in the narrow corridors, muttered dark imprecations, strangled one another on the divine staircases, threw deceiving volumes down ventilation shafts, were themselves hurled to their deaths by men of distant regions. Others went insane . . . The Vindica-tions do exist (I have seen two of them, which refer to persons in the future, persons perhaps not imaginary), but those who went in quest of them failed to recall that the chance of a man's finding his own Vindication, or some perfidious version of his own, can be calculated to be zero.

At that same period there was also hope that the fundamental mysteries of mankind – the origin of the Library and of time – might be revealed. In all likelihood those profound mysteries can indeed be explained in words; if the language of the philosophers is not sufficient, then the multiform Library must surely have produced the extraordinary language that is required, together with the words and grammar of that language. For four centuries, men have been scouring the hexagons . . . There are official searchers, the 'inquisitors'. I have seen them about their tasks: they arrive exhausted at some hexagon, they talk about a staircase that nearly killed them – some steps were missing – they speak with the librarian about galleries and staircases, and, once in a while, they take up the nearest book and leaf through it, searching for disgraceful or dishonourable words. Clearly, no one expects to discover anything.

That unbridled hopefulness was succeeded, naturally enough, by a similarly disproportionate depression. The certainty that some bookshelf in some hexagon contained precious books, yet that those precious books were for ever out of reach, was almost unbearable. One blasphemous sect proposed that the searches be discontinued and that all men shuffle letters and symbols until those canonical books, through some improbable stroke of chance, had been constructed. The authorities were forced to issue strict orders. The sect disappeared, but in my childhood I have seen old men who for long periods would hide in the latrines with metal discs and a forbidden dice cup, feebly mimicking the divine disorder.

Others, going about it in the opposite way, thought the first thing to do was eliminate all worthless books. They would invade the hexagons, show credentials that were not always false, leaf disgustedly through a volume, and condemn entire walls of books. It is to their hygienic, ascetic rage that we lay the senseless loss of millions of volumes. Their name is execrated today, but those who grieve over the 'treasures' destroyed in that frenzy overlook two widely acknowledged facts: One, that the Library is so huge that any reduction by human hands must be infinitesimal. And two, that each book is unique and irreplaceable, but (since the Library is total) there are always several hundred thousand imperfect facsimiles – books that differ by no more than a single letter, or a comma. Despite general opinion, I dare say that the consequences of the depredations committed by the Purifiers have been exaggerated by the horror those same fanatics inspired. They were spurred on by the holy zeal to reach – someday, through unrelenting effort – the books of the Crimson Hexagon – books smaller than natural books, books omnipotent, illustrated and magical.

We also have knowledge of another superstition from that period: belief in what was termed the Book-Man. On some shelf in some hexagon, it was argued, there must exist a book that is the cipher and perfect compendium *of all other books*, and some librarian must have examined that book; this librarian is analogous to a god. In the language of this zone there are still vestiges of the sect that worshipped that distant librarian. Many have gone in search of Him. For a hundred years, men beat every possible path – and every path in vain. How was one to locate the idolized secret hexagon that sheltered Him? Someone proposed searching by regression: To locate book A, first consult book B, which tells where book A can be found; to locate book B, first consult book C, and so on, to infinity . . . It is in ventures such as these that I have squandered and spent my years. I cannot think it unlikely that there is such a total book* on some shelf in the universe. I pray to the unknown gods that some man – even a single man, tens of centuries ago – has perused and read that book. If the honour and wisdom and joy of such a reading are not to be my own, then let them be for others. Let heaven exist,

---

* I repeat: In order for a book to exist, it is sufficient that it be *possible*. Only the impossible is excluded. For example, no book is also a staircase, though there are no doubt books that discuss and deny and prove that possibility, and others whose structure corresponds to that of a staircase.

though my own place be in hell. Let me be tortured and battered and annihilated, but let there be one instant, one creature, wherein thy enormous Library may find its justification.

Infidels claim that the rule in the Library is not 'sense', but 'non-sense', and that 'rationality' (even humble, pure coherence) is an almost miraculous exception. They speak, I know, of 'the feverish Library, whose random volumes constantly threaten to transmogrify into others, so that they affirm all things, deny all things, and confound and confuse all things, like some mad and hallucinating deity'. Those words, which not only proclaim disorder but exemplify it as well, prove, as all can see, the infidels' deplorable taste and desperate ignorance. For while the Library contains all verbal structures, all the variations allowed by the twenty-five orthographic symbols, it includes not a single absolute piece of nonsense. It would be pointless to observe that the finest volume of all the many hexagons that I myself administer is titled *Combed Thunder*, while another is titled *The Plaster Cramp*, and another, *Axaxaxas mlö*. Those phrases, at first apparently incoherent, are undoubtedly susceptible to cryptographic or allegorical 'reading'; that reading, that justification of the words' order and existence, is itself verbal and, *ex hypothesi*, already contained somewhere in the Library. There is no combination of characters one can make – *dhcmrlchtdj*, for example – that the divine Library has not foreseen and that in one or more of its secret tongues does not hide a terrible significance. There is no syllable one can speak that is not filled with tenderness and terror, that is not, in one of those languages, the mighty name of a god. To speak is to commit tautologies. This pointless, verbose epistle already exists in one of the thirty volumes of the five bookshelves in one of the countless hexagons – as does its refutation. (A number *n* of the possible languages employ the same vocabulary; in some of them, the *symbol* 'library' possesses the correct definition 'everlasting, ubiquitous system of hexagonal galleries', while a library – the thing – is a loaf of bread or a pyramid or something else, and the six words that define it themselves have other definitions. You who read me – are you certain you understand my language?)

Methodical composition distracts me from the present condition of humanity. The certainty that everything has already been written annuls us, or renders us phantasmal. I know districts in which the young people prostrate themselves before books and like savages kiss their pages, though they cannot read a letter. Epidemics, heretical discords, pilgrimages that inevitably degenerate into brigandage have decimated the population. I believe I mentioned the suicides, which are more and more frequent every year. I am perhaps misled by old age and fear, but I suspect that the human species – the *only* species – teeters at the verge of extinction, yet that the Library – enlightened, solitary, infinite, perfectly unmoving, armed with precious volumes, pointless, incorruptible and secret – will endure.

I have just written the word 'infinite'. I have not included that adjective out of mere rhetorical habit; I hereby state that it is not illogical to think that the world is infinite. Those who believe it to have limits hypothesize that in some remote place or places the corridors and staircases and hexagons may, inconceivably, end – which is absurd. And yet those who picture the world as unlimited forget that the number of possible books is *not*. I will be bold enough to suggest this solution to the ancient problem: *The Library is unlimited but periodic*. If an eternal traveller should journey in any direction, he would find after untold centuries that the same volumes are repeated in the same disorder – which, repeated, becomes order: the Order. My solitude is cheered by that elegant hope.*

Mar del Plata, 1941

* Letizia Alvarez de Toledo has observed that the vast Library is pointless; strictly speaking, all that is required is a *single volume*, of the common size, printed in nine- or ten-point type, that would consist of an infinite number of infinitely thin pages. (In the early seventeenth century, Cavalieri stated that every solid body is the superposition of an infinite number of planes.) Using that silken *vademecum* would not be easy: each apparent page would open into other similar pages; the inconceivable middle page would have no 'back'.

FIRE

Introduction

At last, Fire appears as *the* Element. The final one, the most dangerous, even if, as it was said before, the elemental fire is not the common fire, which is like an image, an approximation of the central and 'true' fire. There are, too, many kinds of fire. Some of them burn to ashes and destroy. Some others, subtler, give life and strength. The fire Moses saw in the burning bush is not the one of Hell. Fire, like blood, is hot, it brings light, and it is the sign of spirit and love, but a high kind of love. If the fire is not understood, or if its seeker is not of the same nature, everything can be burnt and destroyed. So it is not always possible to experience fully the presence of this great fire. Sometimes it is better just to feel it, or to see its reflection. Otherwise, the proud will be disappointed. As we can see, once again, the element is ambivalent. It gives as it takes, as you take or give. But what is always present is light. The essential, beautiful and everlasting light.

The dark fire of desire burns in Sacher-Masoch's *Venus in Furs*, like a fire in the chimney. This fire, shared by different visions of love, illuminates 'Madam Venus' and opens a new space for desire and fantasy, but through a very complex process. Mary Shelley's *Frankenstein* deals with another fire, the fire of hate. This novel is perhaps one of the more violent ones, because the creator and his creature hate each other beyond the limits of life and death. It goes deep into mankind's desire for eternity, but a mock eternity that reveals all the evil sides of us. Unlike Dr Jekyll, Dr Frankenstein wants something he does not understand.

And hence he is punished with his own destruction. The visions of the Desert Fathers move the frontier between madness and sanity. Often the spiritual visions are compared to a fire, a great fire of divine origin. Like the tongues of fire of the Pentecost, it is a strong current pouring down from Heaven to earth. And the aura of a saint reminds us of the process of (dangerous) imitation between man and God, a strange and blasphemous imitation that can be regarded also as a sacred one. Mercy could be the key . . . The hymn from the *Dead Sea Scrolls* talks about mercy, and mercy can be very difficult – sometimes even impossible – to give. But when it occurs, like unexpected rain in a desert land, it washes away all the injuries, insults and betrayals to allow a certain perfection to arise.

The *Rig Veda* goes far back, to the very root of our world and its mystery. The birth of the gods, like a mystery within a mystery, evokes the birth of light. Agni appears to be Fire itself, the personification of one of the greatest symbols of Vedic and Hindu cosmology, and the symbol of sacrifice, but a sacrifice that makes a bridge between men and gods. And here we are: with the *Bhagavad Gita* we reach a new dominion, that is to say the way a man can become a god; and if we understand that Arjuna and Krishna are both sides of the same unique Being, it is easier to know what all this means: divine fire can be like a hidden reality, and it is up to us to conquer and reveal it . . . Love, then, is like the great and dangerous fire, able to kill or to give life. Kahlil Gibran's *The Prophet* tells us about that. Why fire and love? It is melted with blood, too. And the heart is the crucible of love, but there are so many different kinds of love. The one Gibran speaks of does not belong to us . . . Rumi's poems are always enigmatic, following not one but several paths. The 'light of God' can be the lantern that guides you through the miseries of ego and earthly struggles, and Rumi's wisdom enlightens you without the help of reason. Finally, this optimistic conception of love is reflected, in a magnified way, in Tagore's poems. The evocation of Creation and the immensity of a burning sky end in an everlasting beginning, with the energy of a new day. It is the miracle of life rehearsed by the gods themselves for humans' sake.

From the *Rig Veda*:
Hymns to Agni, God of the Sacrifice

I Pray to Agni

1 I pray to Agni, the household priest who is the god of the sacrifice, the one who chants and invokes and brings most treasure.

2 Agni earned the prayers of the ancient sages, and of those of the present, too; he will bring the gods here.

3 Through Agni one may win wealth, and growth from day to day, glorious and most abounding in heroic sons.

4 Agni, the sacrificial ritual that you encompass on all sides – only that one goes to the gods.

5 Agni, the priest with the sharp sight of a poet, the true and most brilliant, the god will come with the gods.

6 Whatever good you wish to do for the one who worships you, Agni, through you, O Angiras, that comes true.

7 To you, Agni, who shine upon darkness, we come day after day, bringing our thoughts and homage

8 to you, the king over sacrifices, the shining guardian of the Order, growing in your own house.

9 Be easy for us to reach, like a father to his son. Abide with us, Agni, for our happiness.

Agni and the Gods

1 Now get dressed in your robes, lord of powers and master of the sacrificial food, and offer this sacrifice for us.

2 Young Agni, take your place as our favourite priest with inspirations and shining speech.

3 The father sacrifices for his son, the comrade for his comrade, the favourite friend for his friend.

4 May Varuṇa, Mitra and Aryaman, proud of their powers, sit upon our sacred grass, as upon Manu's.

5 You who were the first to invoke, rejoice in our friendship and hear only these songs.

6 When we offer sacrifice to this god or that god, in the full line of order, it is to you alone that the oblation is offered.

7 Let him be a beloved lord of tribes for us, a favourite, kindly invoker; let us have a good fire and be beloved.

8 For when the gods have a good fire, they bring us what we wish for. Let us pray with a good fire.

9 So let praises flow back and forth between the two, between us who are mortals and you, the immortal.

10 Agni, young spawn of strength, with all the fires take pleasure in this sacrifice and in this speech.

The Birth of Agni

1 The young mother secretly keeps the boy tightly swathed and does not give him to the father. The people no longer see before them his altered face, hidden by the charioteer.

2 Who is the boy that you are carrying, young woman? The chief queen, not the stepmother, gave him birth, for the embryo grew for many autumns. I saw him born when his mother bore him.

3   I saw him with his golden teeth and pure colour, testing his weapons far from his field, and I gave him the ambrosia that sets one free. What can those who have no Indra, no hymns, do to me?

4   I saw him moving far away from his field, and his fine herd no longer shining brightly. They could not grasp him, for he had been born; the young women became grey with age.

5   Who are they who separate my young man from the cows? They have never had a cowherd, not even a stranger. Let those who have seized him set him free. The man of foresight should drive the cattle back to us.

6   The enemy powers have hidden among mortals the one who is the king of dwellings, himself the dwelling-place of men. Let the magic formulas of Atri set him free; let those who revile be themselves reviled.

7   When Śunaḥśepha was bound for a thousand, you set him free from the stake, for he sacrificed with fervour. In the same way, Agni, set us free from our bonds when you have settled down here, O wise priest of the oblation.

8   For when you grew angry you went away from me; the guardian of the laws told me this. Indra discovered you, for he knows; he taught me, and so I have come, Agni.

9   Agni shines forth with a high light; by his power he makes all things manifest. He overpowers the godless forces of evil magic; he sharpens his two horns to gore the demons.

10   Let Agni's bellowings reach to heaven as piercing weapons to destroy the demons. His angry glare breaks forth in ecstasy of Soma. The obstacles of the godless cannot hold him back.

11   Inspired with poetry I have fashioned this hymn of praise for you whose very nature is power, as the skilled artist fashions a chariot. If you receive it with pleasure, Agni, let us win waters and sunlight with it.

12   'The bull with the powerful neck, increasing in size and

strength, will drive together the possessions of the enemy without opposition.' This is what the immortals said to Agni. Let him grant shelter to the man who spreads the sacred grass; let him grant shelter to the man who offers oblation.

The Child of the Waters (Apām Napāt)

1 Striving for the victory prize, I have set free my eloquence; let the god of rivers gladly accept my songs. Surely the child of the waters, urging on his swift horses, will adorn my songs, for he enjoys them.

2 We would sing to him this prayer well fashioned from the heart; surely he will recognize it. With his divine energy, the child of the waters has created all noble creatures.

3 Some flow together, while others flow toward the sea, but the rivers fill the same hollow cavern. The pure waters surrounded this pure, radiant child of the waters.

4 The young women, the waters, flow around the young god, making him shine and gazing solemnly upon him. With his clear, strong flames he shines riches upon us, wearing his garment of butter, blazing without fuel in the waters.

5 Three women, goddesses, wish to give food to the god so that he will not weaken. He has stretched forth in the waters; he sucks the new milk of those who have given birth for the first time.

6 The birth of the horse is here and in the sun. Guard our patrons from falling prey to malice or injury. When far away in fortresses of unbaked bricks, hatred and falsehoods shall not reach him.

7 In his own house he keeps the cow who yields good milk; he makes his vital force swell as he eats the nourishing food. Gathering strength in the waters, the child of the waters shines forth to give riches to his worshipper.

8   True and inexhaustible, he shines forth in the waters with pure divinity. Other creatures and plants, his branches, are reborn with their progeny.

9   Clothed in lightning, the upright child of the waters has climbed into the lap of the waters as they lie down. The golden-hued young women flow around him, bearing with them his supreme energy.

10 Golden is his form, like gold to look upon; and gold in colour is this child of the waters. Seated away from his golden womb, the givers of gold give him food.

11 His face and the lovely secret name of the child of the waters grow when the young women kindle him thus. Golden-hued butter is his food.

12 To him, the closest friend among many, we would offer worship with sacrifices, obeisance and oblations. I rub his back; I bring him shavings; I give him food; I praise him with verses.

13 Being a bull, he engendered that embryo in the females; being a child, he sucks them, and they lick him. The child of the waters, whose colour never fades, seems to enter the body of another here.

14 He shines for ever, with undarkened flames, remaining in this highest place. The young waters, bringing butter as food to their child, themselves enfold him with robes.

15 O Agni, I have given a good dwelling-place to the people; I have given a good hymn to the generous patron. All this is blessed, that the gods love. Let us speak great words as men of power in the sacrificial gathering.

The Gods Coax Agni out of the Waters

1   [*A god*:] 'Great was that membrane, and firm, which enveloped you when you entered the waters. One god, O Agni, knower of creatures, saw all your various bodies.'

2 [*Agni*:] 'Who saw me? Who among the gods perceived my various bodies? O Mitra and Varuṇa, where are all the fuel-sticks of Agni that lead to the gods?'

3 [*Varuṇa*:] 'We searched for you in various places, O Agni, knower of creatures, when you had entered into the waters and the plants. It was Yama who discovered you with your many-coloured light which shines beyond the distance of ten days' journey.'

4 [*Agni*:] 'I fled because I feared the role of oblation-giver, so that the gods would not harness me to it, O Varuṇa. My bodies entered various places; I, Agni, have ceased to consider this task.'

5 [*Varuṇa*:] 'Come here. Man, who loves the gods, wishes to sacrifice. When you have completed the ritual, Agni, you dwell in darkness. Make smooth the paths which lead to the gods; carry the offerings with a good heart.'

6 [*Agni*:] 'The brothers of Agni long ago ran back and forth on this task like a chariot-horse upon a road. Fearing this, Varuṇa, I went far away. I fled like a buffalo before the bowstring of a hunter.'

7 [*The gods*:] 'We will make your life-span free of old age, O Agni, knower of creatures, so that you will not be harmed when you have been harnessed. Then you will carry the portion of the offering to the gods with a willing heart, O well-born one.'

8 [*Agni*:] 'Give me alone the pre-sacrifices and the post-sacrifices, the nourishing part of the offering; and the clarified butter out of the waters and the Man out of the plants. And let the life-span of Agni be long, O gods.'

9 [*The gods*:] 'The pre-sacrifices and the post-sacrifices will be for you alone, the nourishing parts of the offering. This whole sacrifice will be for you, Agni; the four quarters of the sky will bow to you.'

Indra Lures Agni from Vṛtra

1 [*Indra*:] 'Agni! Come to this sacrifice of ours, that has five roads, three layers, and seven threads. Be our oblation-bearer and go before us. For far too long you have lain in darkness.'

2 [*Agni*:] 'Secretly going away from the non-god, being a god and seeing ahead I go to immortality. Unkindly I desert him who was kind to me, as I go from my own friends to a foreign tribe.'

3 [*Varuṇa*:] 'When I see the guest of the other branch, I measure out the many forms of the Law. I give a friendly warning to the Asura father: I am going from the place where there is no sacrifice to the portion that has the sacrifice.'

4 [*Soma*:] 'I have spent many years within him. Now I choose Indra and desert the father. Agni, Soma, Varuṇa – they fall away. The power of kingship has turned around; therefore I have come to help.'

5 [*Indra*:] 'Varuṇa, these Asuras have lost their magic powers, since you love me. O king who separates false from true, come and rule my kingdom.

6 'This was the sunlight, this the blessing, this the light and the broad middle realm of space. Come out, Soma, and let us two kill Vṛtra. With the oblation we sacrifice to you who are the oblation.'

7 The poet through his vision fixed his form in the sky; Varuṇa let the waters flow out without using force. Like his wives, the shining rivers make him comfortable; they swirl his colour along their current.

8 They follow his supreme Indra-power; he dwells in those who rejoice in their own nature. Choosing him as all the people choose a king, they have deserted Vṛtra whom they loathe.

9 They say that the yoke-mate of those full of loathing is a swan who glides in friendship with the divine waters. The

poets through their meditation have seen Indra dancing to the Anuṣṭubh.

The Mystery of Agni

1   How shall we with one accord give homage to the benevolent Agni Of-all-men? Great light, by his great and full growth he has propped up the sky as a buttress props a rampart.

2   Do not reproach the self-ruled god who gave this gift to me, for I am a simple mortal, while he is the clever immortal, the insightful, most manly and impetuous Agni Of-all-men.

3   The strong bull with sharp horns and seed a thousandfold has a mighty and double tone. As one reveals the hidden footprint of a cow, Agni has declared to me the inner meaning.

4   Let the generous Agni, sharp-toothed with white-hot flame, devour those who break the dear, firm commandments of Varuṇa and the watchful Mitra.

5   Wilful as women without brothers, wicked as wives who deceive their husbands, those who are evil, without Order or truth, have engendered this deep place.

6   O Agni, who makes things clear, who am I, that upon me when I have broken no commandments you have boldly placed like a heavy burden this thought so high and deep, this fresh question with seven meanings for the offering?

7   Let our vision that clarifies through sacrificial power reach him who is the same everywhere; the precious substance of the dappled cow is in the leather-skin of food, and the disc of the sun has mounted to the head of the earth-cow.

8   What of this speech of mine should I proclaim? They murmur about the secret hidden in the depths: when they have opened the mystery of the cows of dawn, like a door upon a flood, he protects the beloved head of the earth-cow, the place of the bird.

9   This is that great face of the great gods, that the cow of dawn followed as it went in front. I found it shining in the place of the Order, moving swiftly, swiftly.

10 As he blazed beside his parents with his open mouth, he thought of the precious hidden substance of the dappled cow. In the farthest place of the mother, facing the cow, the tongue of the bull, of the flame, stretches forth.

11 When questioned I speak reverently of the Order, if I may, trusting in you who know all creatures. You rule over all this, over all the riches in heaven and all the riches on earth.

12 What is ours of this, what riches, what treasure? Tell us, for you understand, you who know all creatures. Hidden is the farthest end of our road, where we have gone as those who fail follow a false path.

13 What are the limits? What are the rules? What is the goal? We wish to go there as racehorses speed towards the victory prize. When will the Dawns, goddesses and wives of immortality, spread over us their light with the colour of the sun?

14 Those whose speech is empty and contrary, insipid and petty, who leave one unsatisfied, what can they say here, Agni? Unarmed, let them fall defeated.

15 The face of the bull, of this deity kindled for beauty, shone forth in the house. Clothed in white, beautiful in form and rich in gifts, he glowed like a home full of riches.

Agni and the Young Poet

1   The dark day and the bright day, the two realms of space, turn by their own wisdom. As Agni Of-all-men was born, like a king he drove back the darkness with light.

2   I do not know how to stretch the thread, nor weave the cloth, nor what they weave as they enter the contest. Whose son

could speak here such words that he would be above and his father below?

3 He is the one who knows how to stretch the thread and weave the cloth; he will speak the right words. He who understands this is the guardian of immortality; though he moves below another, he sees above him.

4 This is the first priest of the oblation; look at him. This is the immortal light among mortals. This is the one who was born and firmly fixed, the immortal growing great in his body.

5 He is light firmly fixed for everyone to see, the thought swiftest among all who fly. All the gods, with one mind and one will, rightly come to the one source of thought.

6 My ears fly open, my eye opens, as does this light that is fixed in my heart. My mind flies up, straining into the distance. What shall I say? What shall I think?

7 All the gods bowed to you in fear, Agni, when you hid yourself in darkness. May Agni Of-all-men save us with his help; may the immortal save us with his help.

The Hidden Agni

1 The one sea with many births, support of treasures, he sees out of our heart. He clings to the udder in the lap of the two who are concealed; the path of the bird is hidden in the midst of the fountain.

2 The buffaloes bursting with seed, veiling themselves have united with the mares in the same stable. The poets hide the path of the Truth; they keep secret their highest names.

3 The two who are made of Truth yet made of magic have come together; they have made a child and given birth to him and made him grow. He is the navel of all that moves and is firm, who with his mind stretches the thread of the poet.

4   For the waves of truth, the refreshing foods, have always clung to the well-born child for reward. Wearing a cloak, the two world-halves made him grow on butter and food and honey.

5   Full of desire, the wise one brought the seven red sisters out of the honey to see. Born long ago, he was yoked in mid-air; seeking a robe to hide him, he found Pūṣan's.

6   The poets fashioned seven boundaries; he who was trapped went to only one of them. The pillar of life's vigour, he stands in the nest of the Highest, among the supports at the end of the paths.

7   Non-existence and existence are in the highest heaven, in the lap of Aditi and the birth of Dakṣa. Agni is for us the first-born of Truth in the ancient vigour of life: the bull – and also the cow.

From *The Desert Fathers*

Sayings of the Early Christian Monks

Visions

1. A brother went to the cell of Arsenius in Scetis, and looked in through the window, and saw him like fire from head to foot. (He was a brother worthy to see such sights.) When he knocked, Arsenius came out, and saw the brother standing there amazed, and said to him, 'Have you been knocking long? Did you see anything?' He answered, 'No.' After talking with him, Arsenius sent him on his way.

2. Daniel used to say that Arsenius told him a story, as if he were speaking of some other man, and it went like this: Whilst a certain hermit was sitting in his cell, a voice came to him which said, 'Come here, and I will show you the works of the children of men,' so he got up and went out. The voice led him out and showed him a black man cutting wood; he made up a large bundle and wanted to take it away, but he could not do so. Then instead of making the bundle smaller, he went and cut down some more wood, and added it to the first, and this he did many times. When he had gone on a little further, the voice showed him a man who was standing by a pit drawing up water; he poured it out into a certain hollowed-out place, and when he had poured the water into it, it ran down back into the pit. Again the voice said to him, 'Come, and I will show you other things.' Then he looked, and, behold, there was a temple, and two men on horseback were

carrying a piece of wood as wide as the temple between them. They wanted to go in through the door, but the width of the wood did not let them do so, and they would not humble themselves to go in one after his companion to bring it in end-wise, and so they remained outside the door. Now these are the men who bear the yoke of righteousness with boasting, and they will not be humble enough to correct themselves and go in by the humble way of Christ, and therefore they remain outside the kingdom of God. The man who was cutting wood is the man who labours at many sins, and who, instead of repenting and diminishing his sins, adds other wickednesses to them. Now he who was drawing water is the man who does good works, but because other things are mingled in his good works they are lost. It is right for us to be watchful in all we do, lest we toil in vain.

3. Daniel the disciple of Arsenius used to talk also about a hermit in Scetis, saying that he was a great man but simple in the faith, and in his ignorance he thought and said that the bread which we receive is not in very truth the Body of Christ, but a symbol of His Body. Two of the monks heard what he said but because they knew of his sublime works and labours, they imagined that he had said it in innocence and simple-mindedness; and so they came to him and said unto him, 'Abba, someone told us something that we do not believe; he said that this bread that we receive is not in very truth the Body of Christ, but a mere symbol.' He said to them, 'I said that.' They begged him, saying, 'You mustn't say that, abba; according to what the Catholic Church has handed down to us, even so do we believe, that is to say, this bread is the Body of Christ in very truth, and is not a mere symbol. It is the same as when God took dust from the earth, and made man in His image; just as no one can say that he is not the image of God, so also with the bread of which He said, "This is My Body" is not to be regarded as a merely commemorative thing; we believe that it is indeed the Body of Christ.' The hermit said, 'Unless I can be

convinced by the thing itself I will not listen to this.' Then the monks said to him, 'Let us pray to God all week about this mystery, and we believe that He will reveal the truth to us.' The hermit agreed to this with great joy, and each went to his cell. Then the hermit prayed, saying, 'O Lord, you know that it is not out of wickedness that I do not believe, so in order that I may not go astray through ignorance, reveal to me, Lord Jesus Christ, the truth of this mystery.' The other two brothers prayed to God and said, 'Lord Jesus Christ, give this hermit understanding about this mystery, and we believe that he will not be lost.' God heard the prayer of the two monks. When the week was over they came to the church, and the three of them sat down by themselves on one seat, the hermit between the other two. The eyes of their understanding were opened, and when the time of the mysteries arrived, and the bread was laid upon the holy table, there appeared to the three of them as it were a child on the table. Then the priest stretched out his hand to break the bread, and behold the angel of the Lord came down from heaven with a knife in his hand, and he killed the child and pressed out his blood into the cup. When the priest broke off from the bread small pieces, the hermit went forward to receive communion and a piece of living flesh smeared and dripping with blood was given to him. Now when he saw this he was afraid and he cried out loudly, saying, 'Lord, I believe that the bread is Your Body, and that the cup is Your Blood.' At once the flesh that was in his hand became bread, and he took it and gave thanks to God. The brothers said to him, 'God knows the nature of men, and that we are unable to eat living flesh, and so He turneth His Body into bread, and His Blood into wine for those who receive Him in faith.' Then they gave thanks to God for the hermit, because He had not let Satan destroy him, and the three of them went back to their cells joyfully.

4. Daniel told a story of another hermit who used to live in the lower parts of Egypt, and who said in his simplicity that Melchizedek

was the Son of God. Now when the blessed man Theophilus, the archbishop of Alexandria, heard of it, he sent a message asking the monks to bring the hermit to him. When he saw him, he realized that he was a man of vision and that everything that he had asked for God had given him, and that he had only said this out of simplicity. The archbishop dealt with him wisely in the following manner, saying, 'Abba, pray to God for me, because I have begun to think that Melchizedek was the Son of God,' and he added, 'It cannot be true, for the high priest of God was a man. But because I had doubts in my mind about this, I sent for you to pray to God for me that He may reveal the truth of the matter to you.' Then, because the hermit had confidence in the power of prayer, he said to him firmly, 'Wait three days, and I will ask God about this and then I shall be able to tell you who Melchizedek was.' So the hermit went away, and returned after three days, and said to the blessed Archbishop Theophilus, 'Melchizedek was a man.' The archbishop said unto him, 'How do you know that, abba?' The hermit said, 'God showed me all the Patriarchs, one by one, and they passed before me one after the other, from Adam to Melchizedek, and an angel said to me, "This is Melchizedek." That is indeed how the truth of this matter appeared to me.' The hermit went away, and he himself proclaimed that Melchizedek was a man, and the blessed Theophilus rejoiced greatly.

5. In that place when Ephriam of holy memory was a boy, he saw in sleep, or by revelation, that a vine was planted on his tongue and it grew and filled the whole earth with very great fruitfulness and so all the birds of the air came and ate the fruits of that vine and spread the fruit further.

6. One of the monks saw in a dream a company of angels coming down from heaven by the commandment of God, and one of them held in his hand a scroll that was written on the inside and on the outside, and the angels said to each other, 'Who is fit to

be entrusted with this?' Then some of them mentioned one man and others another, and others answered and said, 'Indeed those you mention are holy and righteous, but not sufficiently so to be trusted with this thing.' After they had considered many names of the saints, they finally said, 'No one is fit to be entrusted with this except Ephriam.' Then the hermit who was having this vision saw that they gave the scroll to Ephriam. When he got up in the morning, he heard that they were saying, 'Ephriam is teaching, and words flow from his mouth like water from a fountain.' Then the hermit who had seen the vision realized that whatever he said came from the Holy Spirit.

7. It was said about Zeno that when he was living in Scetis he went out of his cell at night, going towards the marshes. He spent three days and three nights there wandering at random. At last, tired out, his strength failed him, and he fell down as though dying when suddenly a little child stood before him with bread and a jar of water and said to him, 'Get up, and eat.' He stood up and prayed, thinking that it was an illusion. The child said to him, 'You have done well.' He prayed a second, and then a third time. The child said again, 'You have done well.' Then the hermit got up, took some of the food and ate. The child said to him, 'As far as you have walked, so far are you from your cell. So then, get up and follow me.' Immediately he found himself in his cell. Then the hermit said to the child, 'Come in and let us pray.' But when Zeno went inside, the other had vanished.

8. John said that a hermit saw in a rapture three monks standing on the edge of the sea and a voice came to them from the other side saying, 'Take wings of fire and come to me.' The first two did so and reached the other shore, but the third stayed where he was crying and weeping. Later on wings were given to him also, not of fire but weak and feeble so that he reached the other shore with great difficulty, sometimes in the water, sometimes over it.

So it is with the present generation: the wings they are given are not of fire; they are weak and feeble.

9. When Macarius was living in the utter desert he was the only one who lived as a solitary, but lower down there was another desert where several brothers lived. One day he glanced down the road and he saw Satan coming along looking like a man, who passed by Macarius' dwelling. He seemed to be wearing a cotton garment full of holes and a small flask hung at each hole. Macarius said to him, 'Hey, mister, where are you off to?' He said, 'I'm going to stir up the memories of the monks.' The hermit said, 'What are these small flasks for?' He replied, 'I'm taking food for the brethren to taste.' The hermit said, 'So many kinds?' He replied, 'Yes, if a brother doesn't like one sort of food, I offer him another, and if he doesn't like the second any better, I offer him a third; and of all these varieties he'll like one at least.' With these words he went on; Macarius remained watching the road until he saw him coming back again. When he saw the devil, he said to him, 'Good health to you.' The other replied, 'How can I be in good health?' The hermit asked him what he meant, and he replied, 'Because they all opposed me, and no one received me.' Macarius said, 'Ah, so you didn't find any friends down there?' He replied, 'Yes, I have one monk who is a friend down there. He at least obeys me and when he sees me he changes like the wind.' The hermit asked him the name of this monk: 'Theopemptus,' he replied. With these words he went away. Then Macarius got up and went to the desert below his own. When they heard of it the brothers took branches of palm to go to meet him. Each one got ready, thinking that it was to him that the hermit was coming. But he asked which was the one called Theopemptus, and when he had found out, it was to his cell that he went. Theopemptus received him with joy. When he was alone with him Macarius asked him, 'How are you getting on?' Theopemptus replied, 'Thanks to your prayers, all goes well.' The hermit asked him,

'Don't your thoughts war against you?' He replied: 'Up to now, it's all right,' for he was afraid to admit anything. The hermit said to him, 'Well, after so many years living as an ascetic, and being praised by all, though I am old, the spirit of fornication troubles me.' Theopemptus said, 'As a matter of fact, abba, it is the same for me.' Macarius went on admitting that other thoughts still warred against him, until he had brought him to admit them about himself. Then Macarius said, 'How long do you fast?' He replied, 'Till the ninth hour.' 'Practise fasting till a little later,' he said. 'Meditate on the Gospel and the other Scriptures; if a bad thought comes to you, don't look at it but always look upwards, and the Lord will come at once to your help.' When he had given the brother this rule, Macarius returned to his solitude. He was watching the road once more when he saw the devil, and he said to him, 'Where are you going this time?' He replied, 'To stir up the memories of the brothers,' and he went on his way. When he came back the saint asked him, 'How are the brothers?' He told him that it had gone badly and Macarius asked him why. He replied, 'They are all obdurate, and the worst is the one friend I had who used to obey me. I don't know what has changed him, but he doesn't obey me any more; he's become the most stubborn of them all. So I have decided not to go down there again or at least not for a very long time.' When he had said this he went away and Macarius returned to his cell adoring and thanking God the Saviour.

10. Macarius wanted to encourage the brothers so he said, 'A little while ago a mother came here with her son who was vexed by a devil, and he said to his mother, "Get up, let us go away from here." But she said, "My feet are so bad that I can't walk away." So her son said to her, "I will carry you." I am amazed at the cleverness of the devil, how much he wanted them to flee from this place.'

11. He also told the brothers about the devastation of Scetis. He said, 'When you see cells built beside the swamp know that the desolation of Scetis is near; when you see trees planted there know that it is at the door; when you see boys there, take your sheepskins and go away.'

12. It happened that Moses, who lived in Petra, was struggling with the temptation to fornication. Unable to stay any longer in the cell, he went and told Isidore about it. He advised him to return to his cell. But he refused, saying, 'Abba, I cannot.' Then Isidore took Moses out onto the terrace and said to him, 'Look towards the west.' He looked and saw hordes of demons standing about and making a noise before launching an attack. Then Isidore said to him, 'Look towards the east.' He turned and saw an innumerable multitude of holy angels shining with glory. Isidore said, 'See, these are sent by the Lord to the saints to bring them help, while those in the west fight against them. Those who are with us are more in number than they are against us' (cf. 2 Kgs. 6:16). So Moses gave thanks to God, plucked up courage and returned to his cell.

13. When he was in Scetis, Moses used to say, 'If we keep the commandments of our predecessors I will answer on God's behalf that the barbarians will not come here. But if we do not keep the commandments of God, this place will be devastated.'

14. One day when the brothers were sitting near him, Macarius said to them, 'Look, the barbarians are coming to Scetis today; get up and flee.' They said to him, 'Abba, won't you flee too?' He said to them, 'I've been waiting for many years for this day when the word of Christ will be fulfilled, "They who take the sword shall perish by the sword" (Matt. 26:52).' They said to him, 'We will not flee either, we will die with you.' He replied, 'That's nothing to do with me; let each one decide for himself if

he will stay or flee.' There were seven brothers there and he said to them, 'Look, the barbarians are nearly at the door,' and they came in and slew them. But one of them fled and hid under a pile of rope and he saw seven crowns coming down and crowning each of them.

15. It was said that Silvanus wanted to go away to Syria but his disciple Mark said to him, 'Abba, I don't want to leave this place, nor will I let you leave. Stay here for three days.' On the third day Mark died.

16. John who had been exiled by the Emperor Marcion, said, 'One day we went into Syria to see Poemen for we wanted to ask him about hardness of heart. But he did not know Greek and we did not have an interpreter. When he saw we were embarrassed, he began to speak in Greek saying, "The nature of water is soft, the nature of stone is hard; but if a bottle is hung above a stone letting water drip down, it wears away the stone. It is like that with the word of God; it is soft and our heart is hard, but if a man hears the word of God often, it will break open his heart to the fear of God."'

17. Poemen said, 'It is written, "Like as the hart longs for the water brooks, so longs my soul for you, O my God" (Ps. 42:1). Indeed, the harts in the desert eat many snakes and when their venom makes them burn with thirst they come to the waters to assuage their burning thirst. It is the same for monks: in the desert, they are burned by the poison of the demons and they long for Saturday and Sunday to come so that they can go to the springs of water, that is, to the Body and Blood of the Lord, to be purified from the poison of the evil ones.'

18. A brother asked Poemen about the words, 'Do not render evil for evil' (1 Thess. 5:15). He said to him, 'The passions work in four stages: first in the heart, then in the face, third in words, fourth in

deeds – and it is in deeds that it is essential not to render evil for evil. If you purify your heart, passion will not show in your expression, but if it does, take care not to speak about it; if you do speak, cut the conversation short in case you render evil for evil.'

19. The holy bishop Basil told this story: In a certain monastery of nuns there was a girl who pretended she was mad and possessed by a devil. The others felt such contempt for her that they never ate with her, which pleased her very much. She took herself to the kitchen and used to perform all the most menial tasks; she was, as the saying is, 'the sponge of the monastery', but in fact she was fulfilling the Scriptures where it says, 'If any man among you seem to be wise in this world, let him become a fool that he may be wise' (1 Cor. 3:18). She wore a rag around her head, while all the others had their hair closely cropped and wore cowls, and she used to serve them dressed like that. Not one of the four hundred ever saw her chew in all the years of her life. She never sat down at table or ate a scrap of bread, but she wiped up with a sponge the crumbs from the tables and was satisfied with the scouring from the pots. She was never angry with anyone, nor did she grumble or chatter, either little or much, although she was maltreated, insulted, cursed and loathed. Now an angel appeared to the holy Piterion, the famous anchorite dwelling at Porphyrite and said to him, 'Why do you think so much of yourself for being pious and dwelling in a place such as this? Do you want to see someone more pious than yourself, a woman? Go to the women's monastery at Tabennisi and there you will find one with a cloth on her head. She is better than you are. While being knocked about by many she has never let her attention turn from God. But you live here alone and let your attention wander about in cities.' So Piterion, who had never left his cell, asked those in charge to allow him to enter the monastery of women. They let him in, since he was well on in years and, moreover, had a great reputation. So he went in and insisted upon seeing all of them.

The woman he wanted to see did not appear. Finally he said to them, 'Bring them all to me, for the one I want to see is missing.' They said, 'We have a sister in the kitchen who is touched in the head' (that is what they call afflicted ones). He told them, 'Bring her to me. Let me see her.' They went to call her, but she did not answer, either because she had heard what was happening or because it had been revealed to her. They seized her forcibly and told her, 'The holy Piterion wants to see you' (for he was famous). When she came in he saw the rag on her head and, falling down at her feet, he said, 'Bless me!' She too fell down at his feet and said, 'Bless me, my lord.' All the women were amazed at this and said, 'Abba, do not let her insult you. She is touched.' Piterion then spoke to all the women, 'You are the ones who are touched! This woman is an amma (which is what they called spiritual mothers) to both you and me and I pray that I may be counted as worthy as she on the Day of Judgement.' Hearing this, they fell at his feet, confessing various things, one saying how she had poured the leavings of her plate over her; another how she had beaten her with her fists; another how she had blistered her nose. So they confessed various and sundry outrages. After praying for them, he left. After a few days she was unable to bear the praise and honour of the sisters, and all their apologizing was so burdensome to her that she left the monastery. Where she went and where she disappeared to, and how she died, nobody knows.

20. The blessed man Paul the Simple, the disciple of the holy man Antony, used to tell this to the monks: I once went to a certain monastery to visit the brothers for spiritual profit, and after talking with them they went as usual into the church to celebrate the holy mysteries. Paul looked at and scrutinized each one of them, so that he might see in what frame of mind he was going in, for he had the gift, which had been given him by God, of looking into the soul of every man, and of knowing what his soul was like, even as we have the power of looking into each other's faces.

He saw that everyone was going in with glorious aspect of soul, each face full of light, and that the angel of each was rejoicing in him. The exception was one whose face was sick and afflicted, and whose whole body was in darkness; devils grasped both his hands, and they were lifting him up and dragging him towards them, and they had put a ring in his nose. Paul saw also that the holy angel of this man was a long way from him, and that he followed after him sadly and sorrowfully. When the blessed Paul saw these things he wept and smote himself upon the breast many times, and sitting down outside the church, he wept unceasingly for the man who had appeared to him in this state. Now those who saw Paul were greatly astonished, especially at his swift change from happiness to weeping and tears, and they asked him, entreating and begging him to tell them what he had seen, for they thought that, though he might be angry with them, he would tell them. They besought him also, with one voice, to go into church with them. But Paul drove them away from him, and he would not let himself be persuaded to do this. So he sat outside the church and held his peace, and cried aloud and groaned about that which had appeared to him.

After a short time, when the service was ended, and they were all coming out, Paul scrutinized each one of them carefully, so that he might see in what manner those whom he had seen go in would come out, and whether it would be with the same countenance as that with which they had gone in, or not. He saw again that man whom he had seen go in, and whose body before he had entered into the church was in darkness, and behold, he came forth from the church with his face full of light, his body white. The devils followed him at a great distance, and his guardian angel was close to him, and walked with him, rejoicing greatly over him. Then the holy man Paul jumped up, and stood there glad and rejoicing, and he cried out and blessed God, saying, 'Hail to the overflowing mercy of God! Hail to His immeasurable goodness! Hail to His rich treasuries! Hail to His pleasure, which is beyond measure!' Then he ran and stood on a raised platform, and cried with a loud voice, saying, 'Come and see how wonderful are the works of God, and how greatly they are to be admired! Come and see Him who desires that all the children of men should live, and should turn to the knowledge of the truth! Come, let us kneel and worship Him, and say, "He alone is able to forgive sins!"'

So all the monks ran to him eagerly to hear what he was saying. When they had all gathered together, the holy man Paul told them the things that he had seen both when they went into the church, and when each of them came out. Then they begged that brother to tell them the reason of that complete change, and of the gladness that God had given him so quickly. The man, being afraid lest he might be rebuked by the blessed Paul, told them the following things about himself, and without any concealment whatsoever. He said, 'I am a sinful man, and for a long time past, even until today, I lived in lust. When I went into the church, I heard the book of the prophet Isaiah read, that is to say I heard God speaking through him and saying, "Wash, and be clean and remove your evil deeds from before my eyes. Hate the things that are evil, and learn to do good, seek out judgement, and pass righteous sentences upon those who are afflicted. And if your sins be red like scarlet, they shall become white as snow. And if ye are willing to hearken to Me, you shall eat of the good things of the earth" (Is. 1:16–19). Now when I had heard these words from the prophet, that is to say, when I had heard God who was speaking by him, I at once repented sincerely, and sighing in my heart I said to God, "You are the God, who came into the world to make sinners live, therefore show in me the things that you have promised by your prophet, and fulfil them in me, even though I be unworthy of them, for I am a sinner. See, I promise, and I enter into a covenant with you, and I will keep this promise deep in my soul, and will acknowledge it so that from now onwards I will never commit such wickedness again, but I will keep myself far from all iniquity, and I will serve you from this day onwards with a clean conscience. Therefore, O Master, from this day, and from this hour, accept me, for I am penitent; and I will make supplication to you, and will remove myself from all sin." Therefore with such promises and covenants as these I came out of church, and I determined in my soul that I would never again do anything that would lessen my fear of Him.' When the monks heard this they cried out with a loud voice and said to God, 'O Lord how great are your works. In wisdom have you created all things! (Ps. 104:24).'

Now therefore, Christians, since we know from the holy Scriptures and from divine revelation how great is the grace God gives to those who truly run to Him for refuge and blot out their former sins by repentance, and also how according to His promise He rewards them with good things and neither takes vengeance according to justice nor punishes them for their former sins, let us not despair. For as He promised by the prophet Isaiah, He will cleanse those who have lived in sin and will make them bright and white like clean wool and snow, and glad with the blessings of heaven. Moreover, God asserts by the prophet Ezekiel that he does not desire their destruction when He says, 'I do not desire the death of a sinner but rather that he should turn from his evil ways and live (Ezek. 33:11).'

From the *Bhagavad Gita*

2

ARJUNA

1   In thy mercy thou hast told me the secret supreme of thy Spirit, and thy words have dispelled my delusion.

2   I have heard in full from thee of the coming and going of beings, and also of thy infinite greatness.

3   I have heard thy words of truth, but my soul is yearning to see: to see thy form as God of this all.

4   If thou thinkest, O my Lord, that it can be seen by me, show me, O God of Yoga, the glory of thine own Supreme Being.

KRISHNA

5   By hundreds and then by thousands, behold, Arjuna, my manifold celestial forms of innumerable shapes and colours.

6   Behold the gods of the sun, and those of fire and light; the gods of storm and lightning, and the two luminous charioteers of heaven. Behold, descendant of Bharata, marvels never seen before.

7   See now the whole universe with all things that move and

move not, and whatever thy soul may yearn to see. See it all as One in me.

8 But thou never canst see me with these thy mortal eyes: I will give thee divine sight. Behold my wonder and glory.

SANJAYA

9 When Krishna, the God of Yoga, had thus spoken, O king, he appeared then to Arjuna in his supreme divine form.

10 And Arjuna saw in that form countless visions of wonder: eyes from innumerable faces, numerous celestial ornaments, numberless heavenly weapons;

11 Celestial garlands and vestures, forms anointed with heavenly perfumes. The Infinite Divinity was facing all sides, all marvels in him containing.

12 If the light of a thousand suns suddenly arose in the sky, that splendour might be compared to the radiance of the Supreme Spirit.

13 And Arjuna saw in that radiance the whole universe in its variety, standing in a vast unity in the body of the God of gods.

14 Trembling with awe and wonder, Arjuna bowed his head, and joining his hands in adoration he thus spoke to his God.

ARJUNA

15 I see in thee all the gods, O my God; and the infinity of the beings of thy creation. I see god Brahma on his throne of lotus, and all the seers and serpents of light.

16 All around I behold thy Infinity: the power of thy innumerable

arms, the visions from thy innumerable eyes, the words from thy innumerable mouths, and the fire of life of thy innumerable bodies. Nowhere I see a beginning or middle or end of thee, O God of all, Form Infinite!

17 I see the splendour of an infinite beauty which illumines the whole universe. It is thee! with thy crown and sceptre and circle. How difficult thou art to see! But I see thee: as fire, as the sun, blinding, incomprehensible.

18 Thou art the Imperishable, the highest End of knowledge, the support of this vast universe. Thou, the everlasting ruler of the law of righteousness, the Spirit who is and who was at the beginning.

19 I see thee without beginning, middle, or end; I behold thy infinite power, the power of thy innumerable arms. I see thine eyes as the sun and the moon. And I see thy face as a sacred fire that gives light and life to the whole universe in the splendour of a vast offering.

20 Heaven and earth and all the infinite spaces are filled with thy Spirit; and before the wonder of thy fearful majesty the three worlds tremble.

21 The hosts of the gods come to thee and, joining palms in awe and wonder, they praise and adore. Sages and saints come to thee, and praise thee with songs of glory.

22 The Rudras of destruction, the Vasus of fire, the Sadhyas of prayers, the Adityas of the sun; the lesser gods Visve-Devas, the two Asvins charioteers of heaven, the Maruts of winds and storms, the Ushmapas spirits of ancestors; the celestial choirs of Gandharvas, the Yakshas keepers of wealth, the demons of hell and the Siddhas who on earth reached perfection: they all behold thee with awe and wonder.

23 But the worlds also behold thy fearful mighty form, with many mouths and eyes, with many bellies, thighs and feet, frightening with terrible teeth: they tremble in fear, and I also tremble.

24 When I see thy vast form, reaching the sky, burning with many colours, with wide open mouths, with vast flaming eyes, my heart shakes in terror: my power is gone and gone is my peace, O Vishnu!

25 Like the fire at the end of Time which burns all in the last day, I see thy vast mouths and thy terrible teeth. Where am I? Where is my shelter? Have mercy on me, God of gods, Refuge Supreme of the world!

26 The sons of Dhrita-rashtra, all of them, with other

27 princes of this earth, and Bhishma and Drona and great Karna, and also the greatest warriors of our host, all enter rushing into thy mouths, terror-inspiring with their fearful fangs. Some are caught between them, and their heads crushed into powder.

28 As roaring torrents of waters rush forward into the ocean, so do these heroes of our mortal world rush into thy flaming mouths.

29 And as moths swiftly rushing enter a burning flame and die, so all these men rush to thy fire, rush fast to their own destruction.

30 The flames of thy mouths devour all the worlds. Thy glory fills the whole universe. But how terrible thy splendours burn!

31 Reveal thyself to me! Who art thou in this form of terror? I adore thee, O god supreme: be gracious unto me. I yearn to know thee, who art from the beginning: for I understand not thy mysterious works.

KRISHNA

32 I am all-powerful Time which destroys all things, and I have come here to slay these men. Even if thou dost not fight, all the warriors facing thee shall die.

33 Arise therefore! Win thy glory, conquer thine enemies, and enjoy thy kingdom. Through the fate of their Karma I have doomed them to die: be thou merely the means of my work.

34 Drona, Bhishma, Jayad-ratha and Karna, and other heroic warriors of this great war have already been slain by me: tremble not, fight and slay them. Thou shalt conquer thine enemies in battle.

SANJAYA

35 When Arjuna heard the words of Krishna he folded his hands trembling; and with a faltering voice, and bowing in adoration, he spoke.

ARJUNA

36 It is right, O God, that peoples sing thy praises, and that they are glad and rejoice in thee. All evil spirits fly away in fear; but the hosts of the saints bow down before thee.

37 How could they not bow down in love and adoration, before thee, God of gods, Spirit Supreme? Thou creator of Brahma, the god of creation, thou infinite, eternal, refuge of the world! Thou who art all that is, and all that is not, and all that is Beyond.

38 Thou God from the beginning, God in man since man was. Thou Treasure supreme of this vast universe. Thou the One to be known and the Knower, the final resting place. Thou infinite Presence in whom all things are.

39 God of the winds and the waters, of fire and death! Lord of the solitary moon, the Creator, the Ancestor of all! Adoration unto thee, a thousand adorations; and again and again unto thee adoration.

40 Adoration unto thee who art before me and behind me: adoration unto thee who art on all sides, God of all. All-powerful God of immeasurable might. Thou art the consummation of all: thou art all.

41 If in careless presumption, or even in friendliness, I said 'Krishna! Son of Yadu! My friend!', this I did unconscious of thy greatness.

42 And if in irreverence I was disrespectful – when alone or with others – and made a jest of thee at games, or resting, or at a feast, forgive me in thy mercy, O thou Immeasurable!

43 Father of all. Master supreme. Power supreme in all the worlds. Who is like thee? Who is beyond thee?

44 I bow before thee, I prostrate in adoration; and I beg thy grace, O glorious Lord! As a father to his son, as a friend to his friend, as a lover to his beloved, be gracious unto me, O God.

45 In a vision I have seen what no man has seen before: I rejoice in exultation, and yet my heart trembles with fear. Have mercy upon me, Lord of gods, Refuge of the whole universe: show me again thine own human form.

46 I yearn to see thee again with thy crown and sceptre and circle. Show thyself to me again in thine own four-armed form, thou of arms infinite, Infinite Form.

KRISHNA

47 By my grace and my wondrous power I have shown to thee, Arjuna, this form supreme made of light, which is the Infinite, the All: mine own form from the beginning, never seen by man before.

48 Neither Vedas, nor sacrifices, nor studies, nor benefactions, nor rituals, nor fearful austerities can give the vision of my Form Supreme. Thou alone hast seen this Form, thou the greatest of the Kurus.

49 Thou hast seen the tremendous form of my greatness, but fear not, and be not bewildered. Free from fear and with a glad heart see my friendly form again.

SANJAYA

50 Thus spoke Vasudeva to Arjuna, and revealed himself in his human form. The God of all gave peace to his fears and showed himself in his peaceful beauty.

ARJUNA

51 When I see thy gentle human face, Krishna, I return to my own nature, and my heart has peace.

KRISHNA

52 Thou hast seen now face to face my form divine so hard to see: for even the gods in heaven ever long to see what thou hast seen.

53 Not by the Vedas, or an austere life, or gifts to the poor, or ritual offerings can I be seen as thou hast seen me.

54 Only by love can men see me, and know me, and come unto me.

55 He who works for me, who loves me, whose End Supreme I am, free from attachment to all things, and with love for all creation, he in truth comes unto me.

14

KRISHNA

1 I will reveal again a supreme wisdom, of all wisdom the highest: sages who have known it have gone hence to supreme perfection.

2 Taking refuge in this wisdom they have become part of me: they are not reborn at the time of creation, and they are not destroyed at the time of dissolution.

3 In the vastness of my Nature I place the seed of things to come; and from this union comes the birth of all beings.

4 Wherever a being may be born, Arjuna, know that my Nature is his mother and that I am the Father who gave him life.

5 SATTVA, RAJAS, TAMAS — light, fire, and darkness — are the three constituents of nature. They appear to limit in finite bodies the liberty of their infinite Spirit.

6 Of these Sattva because it is pure, and it gives light and is the health of life, binds to earthly happiness and to lower knowledge.

7 Rajas is of the nature of passion, the source of thirst and attachment. It binds the soul of man to action.

8   Tamas, which is born of ignorance, darkens the soul of all men. It binds them to sleepy dullness, and then they do not watch and then they do not work.

9   Sattva binds to happiness; Rajas to action; Tamas, over-clouding wisdom, binds to lack of vigilance.

10   Sometimes Sattva may prevail over Rajas and Tamas, at others Rajas over Tamas and Sattva, and at others Tamas over Sattva and Rajas.

11   When the light of wisdom shines from the portals of the body's dwelling, then we know that Sattva is in power.

12   Greed, busy activity, many undertakings, unrest, the lust of desire – these arise when Rajas increases.

13   Darkness, inertia, negligence, delusion – these appear when Tamas prevails.

14   If the soul meets death when Sattva prevails, then it goes to the pure regions of those who are seeking Truth.

15   If a man meets death in a state of Rajas, he is reborn amongst those who are bound by their restless activity; and if he dies in Tamas he is reborn in the wombs of the irrational.

16   Any work when it is well done bears the pure harmony of Sattva; but when done in Rajas it brings pain, and when done in Tamas it brings ignorance.

17   From Sattva arises wisdom, from Rajas greed, from Tamas negligence, delusion and ignorance.

18   Those who are in Sattva climb the path that leads on high, those who are in Rajas follow the level path, those who are in Tamas sink downwards on the lower path.

19   When the man of vision sees that the powers of nature are

the only actors of this vast drama, and he beholds THAT which is beyond the powers of nature then he comes into my Being.

20 And when he goes beyond the three conditions of nature which constitute his mortal body then, free from birth, old age, and death, and sorrow, he enters into Immortality.

ARJUNA

21 How is the man known who has gone beyond the three powers of nature? What is his path; and how does he transcend the three?

KRISHNA

22 He who hates not light, nor busy activity, nor even darkness, when they are near, neither longs for them when they are far;

23 Who unperturbed by changing conditions sits apart and watches and says 'the powers of nature go round', and remains firm and shakes not;

24 Who dwells in his inner self, and is the same in pleasure and pain; to whom gold or stones or earth are one, and what is pleasing or displeasing leave him in peace; who is beyond both praise and blame, and whose mind is steady and quiet;

25 Who is the same in honour or disgrace, and has the same love for enemies or friends, who surrenders all selfish undertakings – this man has gone beyond the three.

26 And he who with never-failing love adores me and works for me, he passes beyond the three powers and can be one with Brahman, the ONE.

27 For I am the abode of Brahman, the never-failing fountain of everlasting life. The law of righteousness is my law; and my joy is infinite joy.

From the *Dead Sea Scrolls*

4Q434, fr. 1

Bless, my soul, the Lord
for all His marvels for ever,
and may His name be blessed.
For He has delivered the soul of the poor,
and has not despised the humble,
and has not forgotten the misery of the deprived.
He has opened His eyes towards the distressed,
and has heard the cry of the fatherless,
and has turned His ears towards their crying.
He has been gracious to the humble by His great kindness,
and has opened their eyes to see His ways,
and [thei]r e[ar]s to hear His teaching.
He has circumcised the foreskin of their heart,
and has delivered them because of His kindness,
and has directed their feet towards the way.
He has not forsaken them amid the multitude of their
    misery,
neither has He handed them over to the violent,
nor has He judged them together with the wicked.
[He has] not [directed] His anger against them,
neither did he annihilate them in His wrath.
While all His furious wrath was not growing weary,
He has not judged them in the fire of His ardour,

but He has judged them in the greatness of His mercy.

The judgements of His eyes were to try them,

and He has brought His many mercies among the nations,

[and from the hand of] men He has delivered them.

He has not judged them (amid) the mass of nations,

and in the midst of peoples He has not judged [them].

But He hid them in [His] . . .

He has turned darkness into light before them,

and crooked places into level ground,

He has revealed to them abundance of peace and truth.

He has made their spirit by measure,

and has established their words by weight,

and has caused them to sing(?) like flutes.

He has given them a [perfect] heart,

and they have walked in the w[ay of His heart],

He has also caused them to draw near to the w[ay of his heart].

For they have pledged their spirit.

He sent and covered them and commanded that no plague [should affect them].

His angel fixed his camp around them;

He guarded them lest [the enemy?] destroy them.

LEOPOLD SACHER-MASOCH

from *Venus in Furs*

I had a charming guest.

Opposite me, by the massive Renaissance fireplace, sat Venus: not, mind you, some *demimondaine* who, like Mademoiselle Cleopatra, had taken the pseudonym of Venus in her war against the enemy sex. No: my visitor was the Goddess of Love – in the flesh.

She sat in an easy chair after fanning up a crackling fire, and the reflections of red flames licked her pale face with its white eyes and, from time to time, her feet when she tried to warm them.

Her head was wonderful despite the dead stone eyes, but that was all I saw of her. The sublime being had wrapped her marble body in a huge fur and, shivering, had curled up like a cat.

'I don't understand, dear Madam,' I cried. 'It's really not cold any more; for the past two weeks we've had the most glorious spring weather. You're obviously high-strung.'

'Thank you for your spring, but no thanks,' she said in a deep stone voice and instantly sneezed two divine sneezes in quick succession. 'I truly can't stand it and I'm beginning to grasp—'

'Grasp what, dear Madam?'

'I'm beginning to believe the unbelievable and comprehend the incomprehensible. I suddenly understand Germanic female virtue and German philosophy, and I'm no longer amazed that you northerners are unable to love – indeed, haven't got the foggiest notion of what love is.'

'Permit me, Madam,' I replied, flaring up. 'I have truly given you no occasion.'

'Well, you—' The divine being sneezed a third time and shrugged with inimitable grace. 'That's why I've always been lenient with you and even visit you every so often although I promptly catch cold each time despite my many furs. Do you recall our first meeting?'

'How could I forget it?' I said. 'You had rich, brown curls and brown eyes and red lips, but I immediately recognized you by the contours of your face and by that marble pallor – you always wore a violet velvet jacket lined with vair.'

'Yes, you were quite enamoured of that attire, and what a good pupil you were.'

'You taught me what love is. Your cheerful divine service made me forget two thousand years.'

'And how incomparably faithful I was to you!'

'Well, as for being faithful—'

'Ungrateful wretch!'

'I won't reproach you. You may be a godly woman, but you're a woman all the same, and when it comes to love you are as cruel as any woman.'

'What you call "cruel",' the Goddess of Love vividly retorted, 'is precisely the element of sensuality and cheerful love – which is a woman's nature. She must give herself to whatever or whomever she loves and must love anything that pleases her.'

'Is there any greater cruelty for the lover than the beloved woman's infidelity?'

'Ah,' she countered, 'we are faithful as long as we love, but you men demand that women be faithful without love and give ourselves without joy. Who is the cruel one here? The woman or the man? On the whole, you northerners take love too earnestly, too seriously. You talk about duties, when all that should count is pleasure.'

'Yes, Madam, but then we have very respectable and virtuous emotions and lasting relationships.'

'And yet,' Madam broke in, 'that eternally restless, eternally unquenched desire for naked paganism, that love that is the supreme joy, that is divine serenity itself – those things are useless for you moderns, you children of reflection. That sort of love wreaks havoc on you. *As soon as you wish to be natural you become common.* To you Nature seems hostile, you have turned us laughing Greek deities into demons and me into a devil. All you can do is exorcize me and curse me or else sacrifice yourselves, slaughter yourselves in bacchanalian madness at my altar. And if any of you ever has the courage to kiss my red lips, he then goes on a pilgrimage to Rome, barefoot and in a penitent's shirt, and expects flowers to blossom from his withered staff, while roses, violets and myrtles sprout constantly under my feet – but their fragrance doesn't agree with you. So just stay in your northern fog and Christian incense. Let us pagans rest under the rubble, under the lava. Do not dig us up. Pompeii, our villas, our baths, our temples were not built for you people! You need no gods! We freeze in your world!' The beautiful marble lady coughed and drew the dark sable pelts more snugly around her shoulders.

'Thank you for the lesson in classical civilization,' I replied. 'But you cannot deny that in your serene and sunny world man and woman are natural-born enemies as much as in our foggy world. You cannot deny that love lasts for only a brief moment, uniting two beings as a single being that is capable of only one thought, one sensation, one will – only to drive these two persons even further apart. And then – you know this better than I – the person who doesn't know how to subjugate will all too quickly feel the other's foot on the nape of his neck—'

'And as a rule it is the man who feels the woman's foot,' cried Madam Venus with exuberant scorn, 'which you, in turn, know better than I.'

'Of course, and that is precisely why I have no illusions.'

'You mean you are now my slave without illusions, so that I can trample you ruthlessly!'

'Madam!'

'Don't you know me by now? Yes, I am *cruel* – since you take so much pleasure in that word – and am I not entitled to be cruel? Man desires, woman is desired. That is woman's entire but decisive advantage. Nature has put man at woman's mercy through his passion, and woman is misguided if she fails to make him her subject, her slave, no, her toy and ultimately fails to laugh and betray him.'

'Your principles, dear Madam—' I indignantly broke in.

'– Are based on thousands of years of experience,' she sarcastically retorted, her white fingers playing in the dark fur. 'The more devoted the woman is, the more quickly the man sobers up and becomes domineering. But the crueller and more faithless she is, the more she mistreats him, indeed the more wantonly she plays with him, the less pity she shows him, the more she arouses the man's lascivious yearning to be loved and worshipped by the woman. It's always been like that in all times, from Helen and Delilah to Catherine the Great and Lola Montez.'

'I cannot deny,' I said, 'that nothing excites a man more than the sight of a beautiful, voluptuous, and cruel female despot who capriciously changes her favourites, reckless and rollicking—'

'And wears a fur to boot!' cried the Goddess.

'What do you mean?'

'I'm familiar with your predilection.'

'But you know,' I broke in, 'you've grown very coquettish since last we met.'

'How so, if I may ask?'

'In that nothing brings out your white body more splendidly that those dark furs, and you—'

The Goddess laughed.

'You're dreaming,' she exclaimed, 'wake up!' And her marble hand grabbed my arm. 'Wake up!' her voice rang firmly.

I laboriously opened my eyes.

I saw the hand that was shaking me, but this hand was suddenly as brown as bronze, and the voice was the heavy whiskey voice of my Cossack, who was standing before me at his full height of almost six feet.

'C'mon, get up,' the valiant man went on, 'it's a cryin' shame.'

'And why a shame?'

'A shame to fall asleep fully dressed, and while readin' a book at that!' He snuffed the guttered candles and picked up the volume that had slipped from my hand. 'A book by—' He opened it: 'By Hegel. C'mon! It's high time we drove over to Herr Severin – he's expectin' us for tea.'

KAHLIL GIBRAN

from *The Prophet*

And she hailed him, saying:

Prophet of God, in quest of the uttermost, long have you searched the distances for your ship.

And now your ship has come, and you must needs go.

Deep is your longing for the land of your memories and the dwelling-place of your greater desires; and our love would not bind you nor our needs hold you.

Yet this we ask ere you leave us, that you speak to us and give us of your truth.

And we will give it unto our children, and they unto their children, and it shall not perish.

In your aloneness you have watched with our days, and in your wakefulness you have listened to the weeping and the laughter of our sleep.

Now therefore disclose us to ourselves, and tell us all that has been shown you of that which is between birth and death.

And he answered:

People of Orphalese, of what can I speak save of that which is even now moving within your souls?

Then said Almitra, Speak to us of Love.

And he raised his head and looked upon the people, and there fell a stillness upon them. And with a great voice he said:

When love beckons to you, follow him,

Though his ways are hard and steep.
And when his wings enfold you yield to him,
Though the sword hidden among his pinions may wound
you.
And when he speaks to you believe in him,
Though his voice may shatter your dreams as the north wind
lays waste the garden.

For even as love crowns you so shall he crucify you. Even as he
is for your growth so is he for your pruning.
Even as he ascends to your height and caresses your tenderest
branches that quiver in the sun,
So shall he descend to your roots and shake them in their
clinging to the earth.
Like sheaves of corn he gathers you unto himself.
He threshes you to make you naked.
He sifts you to free your from your husks.
He grinds you to whiteness.
He kneads you until you are pliant;
And then he assigns you to his sacred fire, that you may become
sacred bread for God's sacred feast.

All these things shall love do unto you that you may know the
secrets of your heart, and in that knowledge become a fragment
of Life's heart.

But if in your fear you would seek only love's peace and love's
pleasure,
Then it is better for you that you cover your nakedness and
pass out of love's threshing-floor,
Into the seasonless world where you shall laugh, but not all
of your laughter, and weep, but not all of your tears.

Love gives naught but itself and takes naught but from itself.

Love possesses not nor would it be possessed;
For love is sufficient unto love.

When you love you should not say, 'God is in my heart,' but rather, 'I am in the heart of God.'

And think not you can direct the course of love, for love, if it finds you worthy, directs your course.

Love has no other desire but to fulfil itself.

But if you love and must needs have desires, let these be your desires:

To melt and be like a running brook that sings its melody to the night.

To know the pain of too much tenderness.

To be wounded by your own understanding of love;

And to bleed willingly and joyfully.

To wake at dawn with a winged heart and give thanks for another day of loving;

To rest at the noon hour and meditate love's ecstasy;

To return home at eventide with gratitude;

And then to sleep with a prayer for the beloved in your heart and a song of praise upon your lips.

RUMI

from *Spiritual Verses*

The Prophet (Peace Be Upon Him) asks Zayd,
'How are you today, and how did you rise?' And his reply:
'I woke up a believer, O messenger of God'

The holy Prophet said to Zayd one morning,
    'How do you feel this morning, my good friend?'

He said, 'A faithful slave.' Again he asked him,
    'If your faith's garden blossomed, where's the sign?'

And he replied, 'By day I have been parched;
    by night I have not slept, from love and fever.

And so I passed through day and night just as
    the spearhead's tip will penetrate the shield.

For on the other side all creeds are one;
    a hundred thousand years is like an hour.

Eternity before and after time
    is one – the mind cannot go there inquiring.'

He said, 'Bring out the souvenir from travelling
    to match your understanding of these realms.'

He said, 'When other people see the sky,
   I see the throne and those who sit in heaven.

Eight paradises, seven hells appear
   to me as clear as idols to the shaman.

I recognize the creatures one by one,
   like wheat among the barley in the mill.

The strangers from the guests of Paradise
   I see like serpents swimming among fish.'

This time has been revealed for this assembly,
   'the day their faces turn to black or white'.

However wicked was the soul before this,
   it was within the womb, concealed from people.

'The damned are damned inside their mother's
      womb,
   their state is known from marks upon the body.'

The flesh – a mother – bears the infant soul;
   death is the pain and trauma of its birth.

The souls of all who've gone before watch out
   to see how that exultant soul is born.

The Ethiopians say, 'He's one of us.'
   The Anatolians say, 'No, he's too fair.'

When born into the spirit-world of grace,
   there is no difference between white and black.

If he is black the Ethiops take him off;
> if he's a Greek the Greeks take him themselves.

Unborn, it is a puzzle for the world,
> for those who know the unborn are but few.

But surely *'he is seeing by God's light'*;
> he has the way beneath his outer skin.

The human seed is white and fair in substance,
> but it reflects both Greek and savage soul.

It colours those who have '*the fairest stature*'
> or drags the other half to deepest hell.

These words go on forever; go on back!
> Let us not miss the caravan of camels.

'*The day their faces turned to black and white*',
> the Turk and Hindu will be known among them.

They are not known when they are in the womb;
> at birth the strong and weak come into view.

'I see, as on the Day of Resurrection,
> all of them face to face as men and women.

So shall I speak or shall I save my breath?'
> Mohammed bit his lip at him: 'Enough.'

'God's Prophet! Shall I tell the assembly's secret?
> I'll show the world today the Resurrection.

Will you allow me to draw back the veils
    and, like a sun, my substance will shine out,

So that the sun will be eclipsed by me,
    that I may show the date-palm and the willow?

I'll demonstrate the Resurrection mystery,
    the precious coin and that with alloy mixed.

Companions of the left with severed hands,
    I'll show their faithless and deceitful colours,

Reveal the seven holes of their deception,
    in moonlight neither waning nor declining.

I shall reveal the woollen cloak of thieves;
    I'll sound the drum and tabla of the prophets.

I'll bring before the eyes of infidels
    clear sight of hell and heaven and what's between.

I'll show the seething reservoir of Kawsar,
    whose sound and water hit their ears and faces.

And those who run around it parched with thirst,
    I shall identify them clearly there.

And now their shoulders rub against my shoulders;
    their screams are penetrating both my ears.

Before my eyes the folk of Paradise
    embrace each other of their own free will.

They visit one another's place of honour,
    and then they plunder kisses from their lips.

My ear is deafened by the noise of sighing
    of wretched men and cries of "I am suffering."

These words are hints and I would speak in depth,
    but yet I fear I might annoy the Prophet.'

He spoke like this, half-drunken and half-mad.
    The Prophet turned his collar up at him.

He said, 'Beware, hold back, your horse is hot.
    When *"God is not ashamed!"* has struck, shame
    goes.

Your mirror has been sprung out of its case —
    how can the mirror contradict the scales?

How could the scales and mirror stop the breath
    to spare someone offence and spare their feelings?

The scales and mirror are the brilliant touchstones
    were you to use them for two hundred years.

If one should say, "Conceal the truth for me,
    display the increase, don't display the loss",

They'll say, "Don't mock your own moustache and
      beard,
    the scales and mirror, counsel and deception!"

Since God has elevated us so that
    through us reality may be discerned,

Or else, if not, what are we worth, young man;
    how shall we be the showcase of the fair?

But put the mirror back inside its case.
    Illumination's made your heart a Sinai.'

'How could the Sun of Truth, the Sun eternal,'
    he said, 'be kept eclipsed beneath an armpit?

It tears the underhand and underarm;
    no madness and no wisdom can survive it.'

He said, 'Put up one finger to your eye –
    the world appears to be without the sun.

A single fingertip obscures the moon
    – this is a symbol of how God conceals.'

Just as the world is hidden by a point,
    the sun becomes eclipsed by one mistake.

You, close your lips and see the ocean's depth –
    God made the ocean subject to mankind.

As Salsabil and Zanjabil's outpourings
    are subject to the Lord of Paradise,

Four streams of Paradise are in our power,
    not from our might but by command of God.

We keep them flowing everywhere we will,
    like magic at the will of the magicians,

As these two fountains flowing from the eyes
   are subject to the heart and soul's command.

If it desires, it goes to poisonous snakes,
   or it may wish to go to take good counsel.

If it desires, it goes to sensual things,
   or it may wish to go to subtle things.

If it desires, it goes to universals,
   or stays within the gaol of partial things.

So all five senses are just like a channel:
   they're flowing at the heart's command and will.

Whatever way the heart is telling them,
   the senses move and trail their skirts behind them.

The hands and feet are in the heart's control
   just like the staff held in the hand of Moses.

The heart desires – and feet are made to dance
   or flee to increase from deficiency.

The heart desires – the hand is brought to book
   with fingers so that it shall write a book.

The hand is subject to a hidden hand –
   from inside this controls the outer body.

If it desires, it is a snake to foes,
   or it may be a comrade to a friend.

If it desires, it is a spoon in food
    or else a mace that weighs a hundredweight.

I wonder what the heart will say to them –
    such strange conjunctions, stranger hidden causes.

The heart must have the seal of Solomon
    that it can hold the reins of all five senses.

Five outward senses are controlled by it,
    five inward senses at its beck and call.

Ten senses and ten limbs and many others –
    you may count up the ones I've overlooked.

Since you're a Solomon in sovereignty,
    O heart, then cast your spell on sprite and demon.

If you are not deceitful in this kingdom,
    three demons will not take the seal from you.

And after that your name will seize the world;
    you shall possess the two worlds like your body.

But if the demons take the seal from you,
    your sovereignty is gone, your fortune dead.

And after that '*O sorrow!*' and '*O servants!*'
    are fixed for you until '*the day of gathering*'.

If you deny your own deceit, how will
    you save your soul before the scales and mirror?

How Servants and Staff Acted Suspiciously towards Loqmān, Saying, 'He Has Eaten the Fresh Fruit Which We Have Brought'

To his own master, Loqmān seemed to be
  one of the feeblest of his serving boys.

His lordship sent his servants to his orchards
  to bring him fruits so he could savour them.

In servant circles Loqmān was a nuisance,
  his face as dark as night, so spiritual.

The serving boys would take enormous pleasure
  in eating all the fruits with greedy relish.

They told their master, 'Loqmān's eaten them.'
  The master was annoyed and cross with Loqmān.

When Loqmān made enquiries of the reason,
  he ventured into speech to chide his master:

'O Lord, the faithless servant,' said Loqmān,
  'is not accepted in the sight of God.

Test all of us, O you who are so generous,
  by filling up our bellies with hot water.

Then make us run around the desert wastes,
  you riding, and us running round on foot.

Then keep an eye out for the evil-doer,
  the acts of *"the revealer of the mysteries"*.'

The master served his servants with hot water;
    they drank the draught and drank it out of fear.

And then he drove them to the desert wastes.
    That group ran up and down and round about.

They all began to vomit in distress;
    the water brought up all the fruit in them.

Loqmān began to vomit from his stomach;
    the purest water gushed from his insides.

Since Loqmān's wisdom demonstrates this point,
    what is the wisdom of the Lord of Being?

'The day on which all secrets are examined',
    something concealed appears from you, unwished
        for.

'Drink scalding water which will rid their bowels'
    of all the veils on things that are revolting.

The fire is used to punish unbelievers
    because the fire is for assaying stones.

So often have we spoken gently to them;
    those stony-hearted ones would heed no warning.

A vein that's badly cut is healed with pain;
    the donkey's head ends up a meal for dogs.

'For unclean women, unclean men', says wisdom,
    and ugly is a proper mate for ugly.

Paulo Coelho: Inspirations

So go and mate with anything you like,
    and be absorbed in it, its form and features.

If light is what you want, be worthy of it!
    If you'd be far away, be vain and distant!

And if you would escape this ruined gaol,
    don't spurn the Friend, *'bow down and come*
    towards Him'.

The Rest of the Story of the Reply of the Prophet (Peace Be Upon Him)

These words are endless. Be upstanding, Zayd;
    tie up Borāq, the steed of rational speech.

As speech reveals the error of your ways,
    it's tearing down the veil of what is hidden,

And God requires concealment for a time.
    Drive off this drummer-boy; close off the road!

Don't gallop; draw the reins. Restraint is better;
    it's better all are happy in their views.

God wishes those who have no hope in Him
    to not avert their faces from His worship.

While there's still hope, they've still nobility.
    A day or two they run beside His stirrups.

He would prefer His mercy shone on all,
    on good and bad, in universal mercy.

God wishes every prince and every pauper
    was full of hope and fearful and was cautious.

This fear and caution are within a veil,
    so that behind the veil they are protected.

Where's fear, where's caution, when the veil is torn?
    The awesomeness of unseen worlds is shown!

Thought struck a youth upon a river-bank:
    'That fisherman of ours is Solomon!

If that's him, why's he on his own, disguised;
    if not, then why the look of Solomon?'

He was in two minds, thinking thoughts like this,
    till Solomon returned as king and sovereign.

The demon fled the throne and left the kingdom;
    the sword of fortune spilled that demon's blood.

And when he put the ring upon his finger,
    the hordes of sprites and demons gathered round.

And men came too to see what they could see –
    among them was the youth who'd had the vision.

And when he saw the ring upon his finger,
    his wonderings and worries went at once.

Suspicion's at its height when something's hidden;
    investigation chases what's unseen.

Imagining the absent one inflamed him;
    when he appeared, imagining dispersed.

If shining heaven is not devoid of rain,
    nor is dark earth devoid of verdant growth.

Because I need the sense *'they trust the unseen'*,
    I've closed the window of this worldly mansion.

If I cleave heaven apart for all to see,
    how could I say, '*Can you see cracks in it?*'

So in this darkness they investigate;
    each person turns his face in some direction.

Awhile the world's affairs are upside down,
    the thief will take the governor to the gallows.

And many a sovereign prince and noble soul
    becomes his servant's servant for a while.

In absence, good and beautiful is service;
    recalling absent ones in service pleases.

The one who stands before the king to praise him
    is what, compared to him who's meekly absent?

The governor who is at the empire's outposts,
    far from the sultan and the royal shadow,

Defends the fortress from the enemy –
    he'll not forsake the fortress for a fortune.

Remote from court and in outlandish outposts,
   he keeps his loyalty like one who's present.

And for the king he's better than the rest
   who serve him there and sacrifice their lives.

The smallest scrap of duty's care in absence
   is worth a hundred thousand in his presence.

Obedience and faith are precious now,
   but after death, when all is clear, they're surplus.

Since absence, absent one and veil are best,
   then close your lips: a quiet mouth is best.

O brother, steal yourself away from words
   for God Himself reveals inspired knowledge.

The sun's face is the witness of the sun.
   'What is the greatest testimony? – God.'

No, I shall speak, for God and all the angels
   and learned men agree in explanation:

'God and the angels and the learned witness:
   there is no lord except the Lord abiding',

Since God has testified who are the angels,
   that they are partners in His testimony.

It is because weak hearts and eyes can't bear
   the beams of light and presence of the sun.

It's like a bat that's given up all hope
    because it cannot tolerate the sunlight.

Be sure, the angels help as we are helpers,
    reflectors of the sun in highest heaven.

We say we've gained this splendour from a sun;
    we've shone upon the weak as did the caliph.

And like a moon that's new or half or full,
    each angel has perfection, light and power.

By rank each angel has from that effulgence
    a three- or fourfold set of wings of light,

Just like the wings of human intellects,
    among which there is so much variation.

The partner of each human, good or evil,
    is just that angel which resembles it.

The bleary-eyed who cannot bear the sun —
    the star is meant for him to find his way.

The Prophet (Peace Be Upon Him) Said to Zayd, 'Do Not Tell this Secret More Plainly than This, and Keep Watch over Your Obedience'

The Prophet said, '*My followers are stars,*
    a *lamp* for travellers, and *for Satan stoning.*'

If every person had the eye and strength
    to take the light of the celestial sun,

Who would have need of stars, O wretched man,
    to give an indication of the sun?

The moon declares to earth and cloud and
        shades,
    'I was a mortal *"but it is revealed . . ."'*

And in my nature I was dark, like you.
    The sun revealed to me a light like this.

Compared with suns, I have a darkness in me,
    but I have light for darkness of the souls.

I'm fainter so that you can bear my truth,
    for you are not a man of brilliant suns.

I'm blended in like vinegar and honey,
    so I can reach the sickness in the liver.

O addict, when you've shaken off your illness,
    leave off the vinegar and feed on honey.

The throne, which is the heart set free from lust –
    now see '*the Merciful sits on the throne*'.

Thereafter God controls the heart directly,
    for now the heart has found the true relation.

These words go on forever – where is Zayd
    that I may warn him not to seek disgrace?

Returning to the Story of Zayd

You'll not find Zayd, for he has disappeared:
    he's fled the shoe rack, and he's dropped his shoes.

And who are you? Zayd could not find himself;
    he's like the star on which the sun has shone.

You'll find there is no sign nor signal of him;
    you'll find no clue along the Milky Way.

The sense and speech of our forefathers are
    suffused within the light of our king's wisdom.

Their senses and intelligences lost
    in wave on wave of *'be arraigned before us'*.

When morning comes it is the time of burden;
    the stars that had been hidden go to work.

God gives sensation to the senseless ones,
    to rings of them, with rings upon their ears.

They dance and wave their hands about in praise,
    rejoicing with *'O Lord You have revived us.'*

Their scattered skin and dislocated bones
    turned into horsemen churning up the dust.

On Resurrection Day the grateful and
    ungrateful change to being from non-being.

Why snatch away your head? Do you not see?
    Did you not turn it first in non-existence?

Your feet were planted firm in non-existence.
    You asked, 'Who will uproot me from my place?'

Do you not see the action of your Lord?
    He is the One who takes you by the forelock.

And so He draws you to all sorts of states
    of which you had no inkling or conception.

Non-being is eternally his servant.
    To work, O demons! Solomon's alive!

The demon fashions bowls '*like water-troughs*'.
    He does not dare refuse or answer back.

See how you are atremble out of fear;
    be sure non-being's also ever-trembling.

And if you're striving after high position,
    it's just the fear your spirit is in turmoil.

For all except the love of God most fair
    is turmoil, even if it's sugar-coated.

So what is turmoil? Going towards death,
    not having plunged into the living water.

The people's eyes are cast on earth and death;
    they doubt life's water with a hundred doubts.

Strive to reduce your hundred doubts to ninety;
    be gone by night or, if you sleep, night goes.

By night's obscurity seek out that day
   and find that darkness-burning intellect.

In evil-coloured night there is much goodness;
   the living water is the bride of darkness.

Yet who can lift his head up out of sleep
   and sow these hundred seeds of inattention?

The deadly sleep and deadly food befriend you.
   The master slept; the night thief went to work.

Do you not recognize your enemies?
   The fiery ones are foes of those of earth.

Fire is the foe of water and her children
   as water is the rival of his spirit.

The water will extinguish fire because
   it is the enemy of water's children.

And so the fire's the fire of human lust
   in which there lies the root of sin and error.

The outer fire may be put out with water;
   the fire of lust will take you down to hell.

The fire of lust is not appeased by water,
   because it has hell's nature in tormenting.

What is the cure for lust? The light of faith:
   'Your light will quench the fire of unbelievers.'

What kills this fire? The light of God Almighty,
    so make the light of Abraham your teacher,

So that your body like a timber frame
    escapes your fire of self, which is like Nimrod.

This fiery lust does not abate with practice,
    but only by abstaining does it lessen.

So long as you lay firewood on a fire,
    how will the fire die down by stoking it?

When you deprive the fire of wood it dies,
    so fear of God pours water on the fire.

How can the fire besmirch the lovely face
    whose cheeks are rouged with '*reverence of*
      their hearts'?

A Fire Breaks Out in Medina in the Days of Omar (May God Be Pleased With Him)

A fire broke out back in the days of Omar;
    it was consuming stones like kindling wood.

It fell on buildings and on dwelling houses,
    and even caught the wings and nests of birds.

And half the city went up in the flames,
    and water boiled in shock in fear of them.

And those who had their wits about them threw
    their water-skins and vinegar on the fire.

The fire was growing stronger in its rage;
   the source that fuelled it was infinite.

The people flocked in haste to Omar's side:
   'We cannot put the fire out with water!'

He said, 'Indeed that fire's a sign of God –
   a flame out of your fire of stinginess.

What's water? What is vinegar? Give bread!
   Bypass your meanness if you are my people!'

The people said, 'We've opened wide our doors;
   we have been liberal and bountiful.'

'You've given out of habit and by custom.
   You have not opened up your hands for God

But all for glory, showing-off and pride,
   not piety and fear and dedication.

Wealth is a seed, don't sow in barren soil;
   don't put a sword in every brigand's hand!

And know the faithful from the hateful ones;
   seek out companions of the truth and join them!

Each person shows a liking for their own.
   A fool alone then thinks he's done good deeds.'

RABINDRANATH TAGORE

from *Selected Poems*

Brahmā, Viṣṇu, Śiva

In a worldless timeless lightless great emptiness
    Four-faced Brahmā broods.
Of a sudden a sea of joy surges through his heart –
    The ur-god opens his eyes.

    Speech from four mouths
    Speeds to each quarter.
    Through infinite dark,
    Through limitless sky,
    Like a growing sea-storm,
    Like hope never sated,
    His Word starts to move.

Stirred by joy,   his breathing quickens,
    His eight eyes quiver with flame.
His fire-matted hair   sweeps the horizon,
    Bright as a million suns.

    From the towering source of the world
        In a thousand streams
    Cascades the primeval blazing fountain,
        Fragmenting silence,
        Splitting its stone heart.

In a universe rampant
With new life exhalant,
With new life exultant,
In a borderless sky
Viṣṇu spreads wide
His four-handed blessing.
He raises his conch
And all things quake
At its booming sound.
The frenzy dies down,
The furnace expires,
The planets douse
Their flames with tears.
The world's Divine Poet
Constructs its history,
From wild cosmic song
Its epic is formed.
Stars in their orbits,
Moon, sun and planets –
He binds with his mace
All things to Law,
Imposes the discipline
Of metre and rhyme.

In the Mānasa depths
Viṣṇu watches –
Beauties arise
From the light of lotuses.
Lakṣmī strews smiles –
Clouds show a rainbow,
Gardens show flowers.
The roar of Creation
Resolves into music.

Softness hides rigour,
Forms cover power.

Age after age after age is slave to a mighty rhythm –
   At last the world-frame
   Tires in its body,
   Sleep in its eyes
   Slackens its structure,
   Diffuses its energy.
   From the heart of all matter
   Comes the anguished cry –
   'Wake, wake, great Śiva,
   Our body grows weary
   Of its law-fixed path,
   Give us new form.
   Sing our destruction,
   That we gain new life.'

   The great god awakes,
   His three eyes open,
   He surveys all horizons.
He lifts his bow,   his fell *pināka*,
   He pounds the world with his tread.
From first things to last   it trembles and shakes
      And shudders.
The bonds of nature are ripped.
The sky is rocked by the roar
Of a wave of ecstatic release.
   An inferno soars –
   The pyre of the universe.
Shattered sun and moon, smashed stars and planets
   Rain down from all angles,
   A blackness of particles

To be swallowed by flame,
Absorbed in an instant.
At the start of Creation
There was dark without origin,
At the breaking of Creation
There is fire without end.
In an all-pervading sky-engulfing sea of burning
　Śiva shuts his three eyes.
He begins his great trance.

MARY SHELLEY

from *Frankenstein*

My present situation was one in which all voluntary thought was swallowed up and lost. I was hurried away by fury; revenge alone endowed me with strength and composure; it moulded my feelings, and allowed me to be calculating and calm, at periods when otherwise delirium or death would have been my portion.

My first resolution was to quit Geneva for ever; my country, which, when I was happy and beloved, was dear to me, now, in my adversity, became hateful. I provided myself with a sum of money, together with a few jewels which had belonged to my mother, and departed.

And now my wanderings began, which are to cease but with life. I have traversed a vast portion of the earth, and have endured all the hardships which travellers, in deserts and barbarous countries, are wont to meet. How I have lived I hardly know; many times have I stretched my failing limbs upon the sandy plain, and prayed for death. But revenge kept me alive; I dared not die, and leave my adversary in being.

When I quitted Geneva, my first labour was to gain some clue by which I might trace the steps of my fiendish enemy. But my plan was unsettled; and I wandered many hours round the confines of the town, uncertain what path I should pursue. As night approached, I found myself at the entrance of the cemetery where William, Elizabeth, and my father reposed. I entered it, and approached the tomb which marked their graves. Every thing was silent, except the leaves of the trees, which were gently agitated by the wind; the night was nearly dark; and the scene would have been solemn and affecting even to an uninterested observer. The spirits of the departed seemed to flit around, and to cast a shadow, which was felt but not seen, around the head of the mourner.

The deep grief which this scene had at first excited quickly gave way to rage and despair. They were dead, and I lived; their murderer also lived, and to destroy him I must drag out my weary existence. I knelt on the grass, and kissed the earth, and with quivering lips exclaimed, 'By the sacred earth on which I kneel, by the shades that wander near me, by the deep and eternal grief that I feel, I swear; and by thee, O Night, and the spirits that preside over thee, to pursue the daemon, who caused this misery, until he or I shall perish in mortal conflict. For this purpose I will preserve my life: to execute this dear revenge will I again behold the sun, and tread the green herbage of earth, which otherwise should vanish from my eyes forever. And I call on you, spirits of the dead; and on you, wandering ministers of vengeance, to aid and conduct me in my work. Let the cursed and hellish monster drink deep of agony; let him feel the despair that now torments me.'

I had begun my adjuration with solemnity, and an awe which almost assured me that the shades of my murdered friends heard and approved my devotion; but the furies possessed me as I concluded, and rage choked my utterance.

I was answered through the stillness of night by a loud and fiendish laugh. It rang on my ears long and heavily; the mountains re-echoed it, and I felt as if all hell surrounded me with mockery and laughter. Surely in that moment I should have been possessed by frenzy, and have destroyed my miserable existence, but that my vow was heard, and that I was reserved for vengeance. The laughter died away; when a well-known and abhorred voice, apparently close to my ear, addressed me in an audible whisper, 'I am satisfied: miserable wretch! you have determined to live, and I am satisfied.'

I darted towards the spot from which the sound proceeded; but the devil eluded my grasp. Suddenly the broad disc of the moon arose, and shone full upon his ghastly and distorted shape, as he fled with more than mortal speed.

I pursued him; and for many months this has been my task. Guided by a slight clue, I followed the windings of the Rhône, but vainly. The blue Mediterranean appeared; and, by a strange chance, I saw the fiend enter by night, and hide himself in a vessel bound for the Black Sea. I took my passage in the same ship; but he escaped, I know not how.

Amidst the wilds of Tartary and Russia, although he still evaded me, I have ever followed in his track. Sometimes the peasants, scared by this horrid apparition, informed me of his path; sometimes he himself, who feared that if I lost all trace of him, I should despair and die, left some mark to guide me. The snows descended on my head, and I saw the print of his huge step on the white plain. To you first entering on life, to whom care is new, and agony unknown, how can you understand what I have felt and still feel? Cold, want, and fatigue, were the least pains which I was destined to endure; I was cursed by some devil, and carried about with me my eternal hell; yet still a spirit of good followed and directed my steps and, when I most murmured, would suddenly extricate me from seemingly insurmountable difficulties. Sometimes, when nature, overcome by hunger, sunk under the exhaustion, a repast was prepared for me in the desert, that restored and inspirited me. The fare was, indeed, coarse, such as the peasants of the country ate; but I will not doubt that it was set there by the spirits that I had invoked to aid me. Often, when all was dry, the heavens cloudless, and I was parched by thirst, a slight cloud would bedim the sky, shed the few drops that revived me, and vanish.

I followed, when I could, the courses of the rivers; but the daemon generally avoided these, as it was here that the population of the country chiefly collected. In other places human beings were seldom seen; and I generally subsisted on the wild animals that crossed my path. I had money with me, and gained the friendship of the villagers by distributing it; or I brought with me some food that I had killed, which, after taking a small part, I always presented to those who had provided me with fire and utensils for cooking.

My life, as it passed thus, was indeed hateful to me, and it was during sleep alone that I could taste joy. O blessed sleep! often, when most miserable, I sank to repose, and my dreams lulled me even to rapture. The spirits that guarded me had provided these moments, or rather hours, of happiness that I might retain strength to fulfil my pilgrimage. Deprived of this respite, I should have sunk under my hardships. During the day I was sustained and inspirited by the hope of night: for in sleep I saw my friends, my wife, and my beloved country; again I saw the benevolent countenance of my father, heard the silver tones of my Eliza-beth's voice, and beheld Clerval enjoying health and youth. Often, when wearied by a toilsome march, I persuaded myself that I was dreaming until night should come, and that I should then enjoy reality in the arms of my dearest friends. What agoniz-ing fondness did I feel for them! how did I cling to their dear forms, as sometimes they haunted even my waking hours, and persuade myself that they still lived! At such moments vengeance, that burned within me, died in my heart, and I pursued my path towards the destruction of the daemon, more as a task enjoined by heaven, as the mechanical impulse of some power of which I was unconscious, than as the ardent desire of my soul.

What his feelings were whom I pursued I cannot know. Some-times, indeed, he left marks in writing on the barks of the trees, or cut in stone, that guided me, and instigated my fury. 'My reign is not yet over' – these words were legible in one of these inscrip-tions – 'you live, and my power is complete. Follow me; I seek the everlasting ices of the north, where you will feel the misery of cold and frost, to which I am impassive. You will find near this place, if you follow not too tardily, a dead hare; eat and be refreshed. Come on, my enemy; we have yet to wrestle for our lives, but many hard and miserable hours must you endure until that period shall arrive.'

Scoffing devil! Again do I vow vengeance; again do I devote thee, miserable fiend, to torture and death. Never will I give up my search, until he or I perish; and then with what ecstasy shall I join my Elizabeth and my departed friends, who even now prepare for me the reward of my tedious toil and horrible pilgrimage!

As I still pursued my journey to the northward, the snows thickened, and the cold increased in a degree almost too severe to support. The peasants were shut up in their hovels, and only a few of the most hardy ventured forth to seize the animals whom starvation had forced from their hiding-places to seek for prey. The rivers were covered with ice, and no fish could be procured; and thus I was cut off from my chief article of maintenance.

The triumph of my enemy increased with the difficulty of my labours. One inscription that he left was in these words: – 'Prepare! your toils only begin; wrap yourself in furs, and provide food, for we shall soon enter upon a journey where your sufferings will satisfy my everlasting hatred.'

My courage and perseverance were invigorated by these scoffing words; I resolved not to fail in my purpose; and, calling on Heaven to support me, I continued with unabated fervour to traverse immense deserts, until the ocean appeared at a distance, and formed the utmost boundary of the horizon. Oh! how unlike it was to the blue seasons of the south! Covered with ice, it was only to be distinguished from land by its superior wildness and ruggedness. The Greeks wept for joy when they beheld the Mediterranean from the hills of Asia, and hailed with rapture the boundary of their toils. I did not weep, but I knelt down, and, with a full heart, thanked my guiding spirit for conducting me in safety to the place where I hoped, notwithstanding my adversary's gibe, to meet and grapple with him.

Some weeks before this period I had procured a sledge and dogs, and thus traversed the snows with inconceivable speed. I know not whether the fiend possessed the same advantages; but I found that, as before I had daily lost ground in the pursuit, I now gained on him, so much so that when I first saw the ocean he was but one day's journey in advance, and I hoped to intercept him before he should reach the beach. With new courage, therefore, I pressed on, and in two days arrived at a wretched hamlet on the sea-shore. I enquired of the inhabitants concerning the fiend, and gained accurate information. A gigantic monster, they said, had arrived the night before, armed with a gun and many pistols; putting to flight the inhabitants of a solitary cottage, through fear of his terrific appearance. He had carried off their store of winter food, and, placing it in a sledge, to draw which he had seized on a numerous drove of trained dogs, he had harnessed them, and the same night, to the joy of the horror-struck villagers, had pursued his journey across the sea in a direction that led to no land; and they conjectured that he must speedily be destroyed by the breaking of the ice, or frozen by the eternal frosts.

On hearing this information, I suffered a temporary access of despair. He had escaped me; and I must commence a destructive and almost endless journey across the mountainous ices of the ocean – amidst cold that few of the inhabitants could long endure and which I, the native of a genial and sunny climate, could not hope to survive. Yet at the idea that the fiend should live and be triumphant, my rage and vengeance returned, and, like a mighty tide, overwhelmed every other feeling. After a slight repose, during which the spirits of the dead hovered round, and instigated me to toil and revenge, I prepared for my journey.

I exchanged my land-sledge for one fashioned for the inequalities of the Frozen Ocean; and purchasing a plentiful stock of provisions, I departed from land.

I cannot guess how many days have passed since then; but I

have endured misery, which nothing but the eternal sentiment of a just retribution burning within my heart could have enabled me to support. Immense and rugged mountains of ice often barred up my passage, and I often heard the thunder of the ground sea, which threatened my destruction. But again the frost came, and made the paths of the sea secure.

By the quantity of provision which I had consumed, I should guess that I had passed three weeks in this journey; and the continual protraction of hope, returning back upon the heart, often wrung bitter drops of despondency and grief from my eyes. Despair had indeed almost secured her prey, and I should soon have sunk beneath this misery. Once, after the poor animals that conveyed me had with incredible toil gained the summit of a sloping ice-mountain, and one, sinking under his fatigue, died, I viewed the expanse before me with anguish, when suddenly my eye caught a dark speck upon the dusky plain. I trained my sight to discover what it could be, and uttered a wild cry of ecstasy when I distinguished a sledge, and the distorted proportions of a well-known form within. Oh! with what a burning gush did hope revisit my heart! warm tears filled my eyes, which I hastily wiped away, that they might not intercept the view I had of the daemon; but still my sight was dimmed by the burning drops, until, giving way to the emotions that oppressed me, I wept aloud.

But this was not the time for delay: I disencumbered the dogs of their dead companion, gave them a plentiful portion of food; and, after an hour's rest, which was absolutely necessary, and yet which was bitterly irksome to me, I continued my route. The sledge was still visible; nor did I again lose sight of it, except at the moments when for a short time some ice-rock concealed it with its intervening crags. I indeed perceptibly gained on it; and when, after nearly two days' journey, I beheld my enemy at no more than a mile distant, my heart bounded within me.

But now, when I appeared almost within grasp of my foe, my hopes were suddenly extinguished, and I lost all trace of him more utterly than I had ever done before. A ground sea was heard; the thunder of its progress, as the waters rolled and swelled beneath me, became every moment more ominous and terrific. I pressed on, but in vain. The wind arose; the sea roared; and, as with the mighty shock of an earthquake, it split, and cracked with a tremendous and overwhelming sound. The work was soon finished: in a few minutes a tumultuous sea rolled between me and my enemy, and I was left drifting on a scattered piece of ice, that was continually lessening, and thus preparing for me a hideous death. In this manner many appalling hours passed; several of my dogs died; and I myself was about to sink under the accumulation of distress when I saw your vessel riding at anchor, and holding forth to me hopes of succour and life. I had no conception that vessels ever came so far north, and was astounded at the sight. I quickly destroyed part of my sledge to construct oars; and by these means was enabled, with infinite fatigue, to move my ice-raft in the direction of your ship. I had determined, if you were going southwards, still to trust myself to the mercy of the seas rather than abandon my purpose. I hoped to induce you to grant me a boat with which I could pursue my enemy. But your direction was northward. You took me on board when my vigour was exhausted, and I should soon have sunk under my multiplied hardships into a death which I still dread – for my task is unfulfilled.

Oh! when will my guiding spirit, in conducting me to the daemon, allow me the rest I so much desire; or must I die, and he yet live? If I do, swear to me, Walton, that he shall not escape; that you will seek him, and satisfy my vengeance in his death. And do I dare to ask of you to undertake my pilgrimage, to endure the hardships that I have undergone? No; I am not so selfish. Yet, when I am dead, if he should appear; if the ministers of vengeance should conduct him to you, swear that he shall not live – swear that he shall not triumph over my accumulated woes and survive to add to the list of his dark crimes. He is eloquent and persuasive; and once his words had even power over my heart: but trust him not. His soul is as hellish as his form, full of treachery and fiendlike malice. Hear him not; call on the manes of William, Justine, Clerval, Elizabeth, my father, and of the wretched Victor, and thrust your sword into his heart. I will hover near, and direct the steel aright.

Acknowledgements

The editor gratefully acknowledges permission to reproduce extracts from the following:

Hans Christian Andersen Fairy Tales translated by Tiina Nunnally. Edited and introduced by Jackie Wullschlager (Penguin Books, 2004). Texts and translator's note copyright © Tiina Nunnally, 2004. Editorial matter copyright © Jackie Wullschlager, 2004. Reproduced by permission of Penguin Books Ltd. 'The Ugly Duckling' from *Fairy Tales* by Hans Christian Andersen, edited by Jackie Wullschlager, translated by Tiina Nunnally, copyright © 2004 by Tiina Nunnally. Used by permission of Viking Penguin, a division of Penguin Group (USA) Inc.

Tales from the Thousand and One Nights translated by N. J. Dawood (Penguin Classics 1954, revised edition 1973). Translation copyright © N. J. Dawood, 1954, 1973. Reproduced by permission of Penguin Books Ltd.

The Prince by Niccolò Machiavelli, translated by George Bull, with an introduction by Anthony Grafton (Penguin Classics 1961, fourth revised edition 1983, 2003). Copyright © George Bull, 1961, 1975, 1981, 1983, 1995. Reproduced by permission of Penguin Books Ltd.

'Forms and Dispositions' from *The Art of War* by Sun-Tzu, translated by John Minford, copyright © 2002 by John Minford. Used by permission of Viking Penguin, a division of Penguin Group (USA) Inc.

'An Expert on the Jewish Question' from *Eichmann in Jerusalem* by Hannah Arendt, copyright © 1963, 1964 by Hannah Arendt, copyright renewed © 1991, 1992 by Lotte Kohler. Used by permission of Viking Penguin, a division of Penguin Group (USA) Inc.

No Easy Walk to Freedom by Nelson Mandela used by kind permission of Pearson Education.

One Hundred Years of Solitude by Gabriel García Márquez, used by kind permission of Agencia Literaria Carmen Balcells.

Nineteen Eighty-Four by George Orwell (copyright © George Orwell, 1949). Reprinted by permission of Bill Hamilton as the Literary Executor of the Estate of the Late Sonia Brownell Orwell and Secker & Warburg Ltd. Excerpts from *Nineteen Eighty-Four* by George Orwell, copyright 1949 by Harcourt, Inc. and renewed 1977 by Sonia Brownell Orwell, reprinted by permission of the publisher.

Fictions by Jorge Luis Borges, translated by Andrew Hurley (Penguin Books, 2000); first published in *Collected Fictions* by Jorge Luis Borges, translated by Andrew Hurley (Penguin Books 1998). Copyright © Maria Kodama, 1998. Translation and notes © Penguin Putnam Inc, 1998. Afterword copyright © Andrew Hurley, 2000. Reproduced by permission of Penguin Books Ltd. 'The Library of Babel' from *Collected Fictions* by Jorge Luis Borges, translated by Andrew Hurley, copyright © 1998 by Maria Kodama; translation copyright © 1998 by Penguin Putnam Inc. Used by permission of Viking Penguin, a division of Penguin Group (USA) Inc. From *Collected Fictions* by Jorge Luis Borges, copyright © Maria Kodama, 1998. Translation and notes copyright © Penguin

Putnam Inc., 1998. Reprinted by permission of Penguin Group (Canada), a Division of Pearson Canada Inc.

The Rig Veda: An Anthology of One Hundred and Eight Hymns selected, translated and annotated by Wendy Doniger O'Flaherty (Penguin Classics, 1981). Copyright © Wendy Doniger O'Flaherty, 1981. Reproduced by permission of Penguin Books Ltd.

The Desert Fathers translated with an introduction by Benedicta Ward (Penguin Books, 2003). Copyright © Benedicta Ward, 2003. Reproduced by permission of Penguin Books Ltd.

The Bhagavad Gita translated with an introduction by Juan Mascaró (Penguin Classics, 1962). Copyright © Juan Mascaró, 1962. Reproduced by permission of Penguin Books Ltd.

The Complete Dead Sea Scrolls in English by Geza Vermes (Penguin Books, 2004). Copyright © Geza Vermes, 1962, 1965, 1968, 1975, 1995, 1997, 2004. Reproduced by permission of Penguin Books Ltd.

Venus in Furs by Leopold von Sacher-Masoch, translated by Joachim Neugroschel, copyright © 2000 by Joachim Neugroschel. Used by permission of Penguin, a division of Penguin Group (USA) Inc.

Spiritual Verses by Rumi, translated by Alan Williams (Penguin Books, 2006). Translation copyright © Alan Williams, 2006. Reproduced by permission of Penguin Books Ltd.

Rabindranath Tagore: Selected Poems translated by William Radice (Penguin, 1985). Copyright © William Radice, 1985. Reproduced by permission of Penguin Books Ltd.

Acknowledgements

Every effort has been made to trace and contact the copyright-holders prior to publication. If notified, the publisher undertakes to rectify any errors or omissions at the earliest opportunity.